INVESTING IN EMERGING GROWTH STOCKS

INVESTING IN EMERGING GROWTH STOCKS

Making Money with Tomorrow's Blue Chips

James W. Broadfoot III

JOHN WILEY & SONS

New York   Chichester   Brisbane   Toronto   Singapore

Library of Congress Cataloging-in-Publication Data

Broadfoot, James W.
  Investing in emerging growth stocks / James W. Broadfoot III.
    p. cm.
  Bibliography: p.
  Includes index.
  ISBN 0-471-61844-6
  1. Stocks. 2. Investments. I. Title.
HG4661.B76 1989
332.63'22—dc19   88-29021
                                                          CIP

Printed in the United States of America

10 9 8 7 6 5 4 3 2

With love,
For Michèle, Francesca and Elliot,
and the angels.

Foreword

"Great oaks from little acorns grow." Although the proverb probably didn't originate as a comment on American capitalism, it applies especially well to our system of business. The building of great industries is part of the unique destiny of the United States. So deeply rooted in our heritage is the aspiration for growth that we sometimes forget that not all nations share this cultural characteristic. And it is a trait that is important for our continued prosperity. Most of the new jobs being created in the United States are in businesses with fewer than 100 employees. It is the emerging growth companies that are driving America's future.

Investing in emerging growth companies is not only good for our country; it is also good for the investor. As Jim Broadfoot reminds us, "Almost every one of today's largest and strongest corporations was once an emerging growth company." Obviously, owning shares in such growing businesses is a powerful way to increase your personal wealth.

But, as many investors have found, discovering the small company that is destined to become a corporate titan is not easy. Information about smaller firms is often hard to come by; gauging the prospects of a potential investment can be difficult. That is where *Investing in Emerging Growth Stocks* comes in. In this book, Jim Broadfoot guides the investor through the process of systematically analyzing smaller companies so as to find those with the potential for enormous growth. His approach demystifies the investment process through numerous examples and a refreshingly practical, common-sense style.

Jim Broadfoot's background has equipped him marvelously well to create this book. His educational preparation, career in business, and distinguished record as an investment analyst and advisor have combined to give him both practical and theoretical knowledge of the emerging growth field. Furthermore, Jim is gifted with the ability to present sophisticated concepts and methods in an understandable, interesting way, in a style light on jargon and buzz words, but heavy on insights.

I find the case studies Jim offers especially fascinating. I expect to be using the book often myself, as a check on my own investment thinking—how does my analysis compare with Jim's? You'll be doing the same, I'm sure.

The emerging growth field is appealing because almost any investor can identify with the dream of rapid growth. With Jim Broadfoot's help, you'll have a better chance of turning your own dreams into realities. I wish you many happy acorns!

THOMAS C. BARRY
President and Chief Executive Officer
Rockefeller & Company, Inc.

Preface

This book is about making money in the stock market by investing in small, fast-growing companies—emerging growth stocks. I first became seriously interested in this subject when I was studying for an MBA in finance. At Wharton, I found that past stock prices represent a huge, ever-growing storehouse of data that's like a gold mine for academics who want to test new theories of finance. My notebooks were soon filled with funny-looking little symbols and esoteric equations. You would have thought I was studying astrophysics instead of trying to learn about the stock market.

When I began my career as a securities analyst, I found that everything I knew about the Efficient Market Hypothesis and other theories was useful but mainly as background information. What I really needed was a way to pick stocks that had a good chance of going up more than the market and to avoid stocks that might go down a lot. That's what I was being paid for. I had some vague notions of how to go about doing it and received quite a bit of help from a few veterans. But most of what I know today is based on experience. I've always tried to learn by analyzing my mistakes as well as my successful investments.

When I was starting out, I certainly could have used more practical, down-to-earth guidance than the stuff I had learned in school. That's why I've written this book. It's not based on any statistical research or empirical evidence; just 15 years of actual experience. It offers the kind of advice that would have saved me a lot of mistakes and a lot of money if it had been available when I was starting my career.

I've written the book as much for individual investors as for future securities analysts. There are probably thousands and thousands of individual investors who've been soured on emerging growth investing because they've never fully understood it. Even though it's a simple, straightforward philosophy, there are a lot of subtleties that make it difficult to implement effectively. Unaware of these factors, many individual investors just take an occasional flyer on some highly speculative small stock. They haven't done any real analysis; they usually don't know what to look for anyway; and they don't have any diversification within the emerging growth sector. So they usually get burned. After this happens a few times, they give up on emerging growth investing because it seems too risky. This is unfortunate because the problem is with the execution, not the philosophy. Hopefully this book will keep some investors from unnecessarily giving up the high returns that are possible with long-term investments in emerging growth stocks.

Throughout this book I have used only masculine personal pronouns to keep the flow of the narrative as smooth as possible, and as a matter of convenience. It is not my intention to slight in any way the many women who are active participants in the world of finance.

Although this book presents sound investment strategies that will help any emerging growth investor, some readers may still feel a need for advice that's more specific and timely than can be delivered in a book format. For these readers, I recommend a subscription to *The Emerging Growth Investor*. This monthly newsletter offers stock recommendations and investment advice based on the same principles advocated in this book. For subscription information, simply drop a line to:

Emerging Growth Publications
P.O. Box 39211
Baltimore, MD 21212-9211

I never could have written the book without the enormous support and encouragement provided by my wife, Michèle. Many thanks also to my friends Steve Boesel and Bob Hall for reading the original manuscript. Their suggestions helped me make a lot of improvements.

JAMES W. BROADFOOT III

Baltimore, Maryland
March 1989

Contents

Introduction

The idea of investing in small, rapidly growing companies has enormous appeal because it can be so rewarding. Almost everyone has heard stories about investors who have made small fortunes buying stock in great companies when they were still very small and not yet well known, and most of their growth as well as stock appreciation was still ahead of them. But this is a difficult and risky style of investing; many small companies falter and never produce the kind of growth that is expected of them.

This book is written for investors who would like to be more active in the emerging growth sector of the stock market but are wary of the risks and feel they have to know more about this style of investing to be comfortable with it. It will lead you through every aspect of the investment process, along the way developing guidelines to help you realize the high returns that are possible from emerging growth stocks. These guidelines will also help you avoid the high risks often associated with emerging growth—but they aren't ironclad rules, and there's certainly nothing magical about them. They may even encourage you to pass up a winner from time to time, and they may cause you to miss an occasional buying opportunity. But averaged out over the long term, they'll keep you out of trouble. This is most important because emerging growth investing is risky and provides plenty of opportunities to lose money.

We'll start by putting the emerging growth style into perspective—comparing it with other investment approaches, examining its risks and rewards, and analyzing one company whose continued success has recently propelled it beyond the emerging growth category. This will help you in deciding how suitable emerging growth stocks are as part of the answer to your overall investment needs.

Almost as important a question is when to invest in emerging growth stocks. Recognizing the best times to play and the best times to stay on the sidelines is a key way to reduce risk and improve the odds of success. We'll address this issue by examining the valuation cycles of the T. Rowe Price New Horizons Fund, which is the best available proxy for the emerging growth universe. The relationship of this fund's price/earnings (P/E) ratio to the Standard & Poor's 500 has been an excellent indicator of emerging growth values, but it has been difficult to use effectively because investor psychology often gets in the way.

Next, we'll turn to stock selection, which is really the backbone of the emerging growth investment process. This is one area where the individual investor has a real advantage relative to mutual funds or other institutional investors; smaller size makes it possible to be a lot more particular in deciding which stocks to own. We'll examine some basic standards that can help in the winnowing out process: why it's best to stick with companies that operate in a fertile industry environment, companies that have limited competition, and companies that can finance most of their growth internally. And then we'll see why it's necessary to go beyond these basics as we examine the business characteristics that make many small fast-growing companies prone to fundamental disappointments.

By analyzing two companies that met all the standard criteria but were tripped up by some common problems, we'll see what to avoid as well as what to look for in evaluating emerging growth investments. We'll also examine the enormous strain that rapid growth places on small companies and diagnose the factors that give some of them an edge in being able to cope with it. We'll see how companies that have good visibility, such as provided by a base of recurring revenue, are the most manageable and the least likely to stumble and disappoint investors. And finally we'll take a look at the ingredients necessary to produce really big winners. The leverage that creates these home-run stocks is usually the result of a potent combination: rising profit margins, favorable earnings surprises, and expanding P/E ratios. We'll discuss some methods that can help you identify these stocks ahead of time.

Although good stock selection is critical, it's also essential to consider valuation. You can have a portfolio full of fine little companies that consistently come through with strong earnings growth, but your returns won't be very good unless you buy them at reasonable prices. So we'll discuss the best way of comparing emerging growth stocks in terms of valuation. And we'll analyze the serious error that most investors make: overemphasizing P/E risk and underemphasizing fundamental risk. Often the best performing stocks in an emerging growth portfolio are those with the highest P/E ratios because they deliver earnings growth and don't disappoint investors. We'll see why some principles that work well for value investors can't be carried over to emerging growth. If you try to buy growth for the lowest possible P/E ratio, you'll often end up with a portfolio full of junk.

Next, we'll talk about buying and selling. Once you've decided on the stocks you want to own and a reasonable price to pay for them, you still have to make the trades. For most investors, this means no more than calling their broker. But emerging growth stocks are quite illiquid and therefore are volatile. We'll examine how this occasionally creates trading opportunities that can work in your favor. And we'll also discuss some strategies that can help make you a better seller. Because these stocks carry above-average fundamental risk, mistakes are inevitable—no matter how painstakingly careful you are in making your selections. So selling is a part of the investment process that you can't afford to ignore.

And finally, we'll take a step closer to putting theory into practice with a number of case studies of successful emerging growth companies.

I believe successful investing is as much art as science. Anybody can learn to run a spreadsheet program, but developing "a feel for the deal" is something else. It requires good judgment, something that usually comes only with experience. Here I'll share with you many of my experiences as a professional investor. These are the basis for the strategy I've designed to give you an edge in implementing this very exciting investment style.

Wherever possible, I have illustrated points with examples of stocks I've either owned or recommended, for better or worse. As you read them, remember that investors must continually deal with change, and this is particularly true in the world of emerging growth. A company that's described here to illustrate some positive characteristic may have faltered in the meantime. So please don't interpret specific company references or case studies as anything more than examples used to make a point. And not all of the examples are positive. Hopefully, the negative ones will allow you to profit from some of my mistakes, which is certainly less expensive than learning from your own.

Part I
Whether to Play, When to Play

1

The Promise of
Emerging Growth

Emerging growth is an investment style that no serious investor can afford to ignore. The one essential reason for considering it as a part of any investment program is that it can yield very high returns—both in absolute terms and relative to the overall stock market. For instance, the T. Rowe Price New Horizons Fund, which is probably the best available proxy for the emerging growth sector of the stock market, had an average annual return of 25.2% over the 8 years from 1965 through 1972. This compared to only 7.7% for the overall market, as measured by the S&P 500. In the 6 years from 1977 through 1982 New Horizons' annual return was 22.0% versus 10.2% for the S&P. We're not talking about a few percentage points, likely as not random, measured over a brief period of time. Rather, these are significant differences that have occurred over intervals that are quite long by most investors' standards. Figure 1.1 shows in graphic terms just how big the premiums from emerging growth stocks were during these two periods.

Yet emerging growth is not an appropriate style for all investors because it involves above average risk, just as it holds out the promise of above average rewards. This risk is partially due to the fundamental characteristics of emerging growth companies themselves; and in part it is attributable to cycles of performance that affect this entire sector of the market. Although emerging growth stocks have enjoyed some long periods of

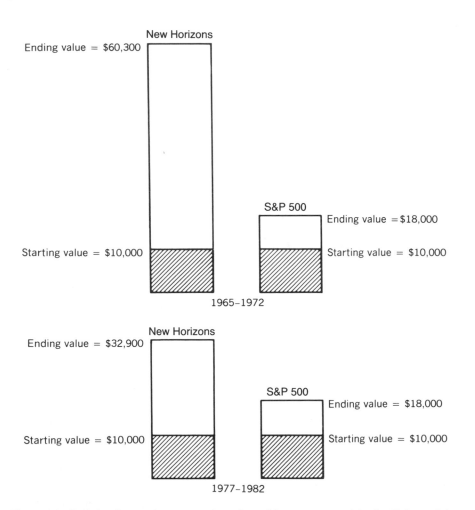

Figure 1.1. Comparative performance: the value of $10,000 invested in the T. Rowe Price New Horizons Fund (a good proxy for emerging stocks in general) versus the S&P 500. Courtesy of T. Rowe Price Associates, Inc.

superior performance, there have also been times when they have substantially lagged behind the overall market.

The most recent period of underperformance started in the second half of 1983 and has continued through 1988. In the past, long periods of poor relative performance have always set the stage for powerful upcycles. So this may be an excellent time for you to give serious consideration to including emerging growth stocks as part of your overall investment strategy.

INVESTMENT STYLES

Every investor thinks of stock prices in terms of two variables—earnings and P/E ratio. Or, in equation form:

$$Price = Earnings \times P/E \ Ratio$$

Investment styles differ primarily according to which variable they emphasize.

Essentially there are two basic styles of investing, with a lot of variations in between. Value investors are at one extreme. They focus heavily on a stock's P/E ratio and pay relatively less attention to the earnings part of the equation. Value investors prefer to pay a very low multiple of earnings (P/E ratio) for a stock. This limits their downside risk, provided the earnings don't collapse.

Value investors also like to buy stocks that seem underpriced in terms of their P/E ratio. They expect to benefit from the price appreciation that will eventually occur if the market wakes up and realizes the stock deserves to sell at a more realistic (higher) multiple. And they also tend to favor stocks that have high dividend yields and stocks that sell at or below their book value—two more factors that help to limit downside risk.

The value style is popular with many investors because it is conservative and emphasizes preservation of capital. In addition, a number of investors have compiled excellent long-term records by following this philosophy. One of the most notable is Warren Buffet, a disciple of the legendary Benjamin Graham, who literally wrote the book on this approach to investing. Also David Dreman and Mario Gabelli are among the better known advocates of value investing.

At the opposite end of the spectrum is growth investing. This is a more aggressive, higher risk style that places primary emphasis on the earnings part of the equation. Growth investors don't ignore P/E ratios any more than value investors ignore earnings, but their first question will probably be how fast are the earnings growing, not what multiple does the stock sell for.

Growth investors believe that whether earnings are paid out to shareholders as dividends or ploughed back into the business to finance future growth, they are critical in determining what a share of stock is worth. Because they consider earnings so important, growth investors expect that over a long period of time the price of a company's stock will rise or fall roughly in line with its earnings. So their portfolios are heavily weighted with companies they expect to experience strong earnings growth. Probably the greatest proponent of growth stock investing was the late T. Rowe Price, who some 50 years ago founded an investment counsel firm based on this philosophy.

Emerging growth investing is really nothing more than the growth stock philosophy taken to its extreme. Because emerging growth investors believe that stock prices are driven by earnings, they seek out the companies that can provide the highest rate of earnings growth. And their search for the fastest growing companies inevitably draws them toward small companies.

Small companies enjoy several advantages that allow them to grow faster than larger companies. The most obvious is that a fast-growing product or service has a much greater impact on a small company. For instance, if a company starts with a base of $40 million, an additional $10 million of sales translates into a growth rate of 25%. But the same $10 million increment represents a growth rate of just 2% for a company with a starting base of $500 million. And for a company that's already doing $5 billion of revenue, it almost gets lost in the rounding.

Small companies also derive an important advantage from the fact that their business is usually concentrated in just one product line. They are not burdened by mature, slow-growing divisions that act as a drag on their overall growth rate. This tight focus also makes small companies purer investment plays on the particular market segment they specialize in. For instance, if you're looking for the most direct way to invest in the fast-growing personal computer market, you will buy stock in MicroSoft or Lotus, rather than IBM. The reason is simply that these smaller companies' business is totally concentrated in just this one segment of the overall computer market. Similarly, Jiffy Lube, rather than Quaker State, is the purest investment play on the fast-growing market for quick oil changes because this is its only business.

Probably the most important single advantage enjoyed by small companies relates to the work atmosphere they can foster. It starts with the fact that key employees are usually large shareholders. This gives them plenty of motivation for finding innovative ways of doing their jobs and achieving high levels of productivity. The big payoff for them is not through salary, but stock appreciation. So an engineer at a small high-tech company, for instance, is likely to put in a little more effort and work longer hours than his counterpart at a larger company.

But it is more than just financial incentive that motivates small company employees. If you are 1 of 40 employees, instead of 1 of 40,000, you are likely to feel a greater sense of involvement and commitment to the organization. And knowing everyone is important, too, because it makes communication a lot simpler and more direct. There are fewer opportunities for committees and other forms of bureaucratic inertia to creep into the organization. This helps small companies to stay flexible, and to move quickly in exploiting new business opportunities as they develop. They are often faster than big companies in adapting to technological change, and more nimble in bringing new products to market.

All of these advantages make it possible for small companies to achieve very high rates of growth, and this is what attracts emerging growth investors to them. Nevertheless, the vast majority of small companies aren't emerging growth companies at all. More often, they are small and destined to remain small because they are undistinguished participants in mature industries that are crowded and highly competitive. To grow rapidly, a small company must also operate in a fertile business environment—technology, health care, business services, leisure, or specialty retailing for instance. The very best emerging growth companies are usually ones that have actually created their own niche within such an industry. As a result, their business is proprietary, and they have little or no direct competition. This allows them to earn high profit margins, so they can finance most of their growth internally. Companies with these characteristics can provide long-term investors with very high returns.

EMERGING GROWTH COMPANIES

Almost every one of today's largest and strongest corporations was once an emerging growth company. Many of the blue chip stocks that make up the Dow Jones Industrials are a century or more old, so it is hard to imagine them as small companies. But there are also a number of very prominent companies that are young enough to still be run by their founders—Digital Equipment and Wal-Mart Stores, for example. And several of the men running McDonald's today first went to work there when it was still tiny and unknown. Of course, the hope of every emerging growth investor is to discover one of these great companies when it is very young and most of its growth and stock appreciation still lie ahead.

To get a better idea of what a successful emerging growth company is like, let's take a look at a specific example of one that has just recently outgrown this classification: Computer Associates. This company's primary business is the development and marketing of software for IBM mainframe computers. It has compiled a very impressive record of sales and earnings growth and in the process has rewarded its shareholders handsomely.

Year Ending 3/31	1983	1984	1985	1986	1987
Revenue ($ Millions)	$58.1	$84.7	$128.9	$191.0	$309.3
Earnings per Share	$.15	$.22	$.29	$.41	$.74
Percentage Increase	67%	47%	32%	41%	80%

Computer Associates has obviously grown at a very high rate, but its record is also notable because of the consistency of this growth. In fact, the company has never experienced a down quarter since 1981, when it first became publicly owned. A record like this—one of both growth *and* consistency—is the kind that investors will eventually reward with a high P/E ratio, as they become increasingly confident that past success can be extended into the future. And this can lead to excellent gains. If you do a good job of buying this kind of stock, you can benefit from the potent combination of high growth and an expanding multiple—a combination that can leverage your return up to a very high level.

Let's look at the factors that have allowed Computer Associates to achieve such a fine record. First, it operates in a very favorable business environment. The company's base of potential customers consists of the thousands of IBM mainframe users throughout the world, to whom it offers over 20 different systems software packages. This market is very large, and it's still growing. Moreover, the kind of software Computer Associates specializes in—products designed to improve the productivity of either the machines themselves or the programmers—is relatively easy to sell. There has been a chronic shortage of programmers for almost as long as there have been computers, so it's usually not hard to convince prospective customers of the need for products that help solve this problem and, at the same time, make their lives easier. These factors create a business environment that doesn't guarantee high growth by itself but is certainly very conducive to it.

To take full advantage of the opportunities its market offers, Computer Associates has followed a strategy of continually broadening its product line, both through internal development and acquisitions. This enables its sales force—one of the best in the business—to keep going back to the user base over and over again with new products. Sales to existing customers are naturally much easier to make than sales to new prospects, who are less familiar with the quality of the company's products and the level of support it offers its users.

And to make these existing users even juicier targets for follow-on sales, Computer Associates has taken great care to keep all of its software packages fully integrated. This means they are designed to be compatible and work smoothly with one another. So for an existing user it's much easier to get up and running with a Computer Associates product than with a competitor's. This feature provides an important edge in competing against stand-alone products that are roughly equivalent in terms of price and performance.

Most of Computer Associates' software packages sell for under $10,000, a relatively low price in the world of IBM mainframes. The important thing about this price level is that it's low enough so that most customers can make the purchase without review and approval by corporate committees. Being able to bypass these reviews is particularly helpful when capital spending budgets are under pressure. This is the main reason why Computer Associates has not been plagued by the lengthening sales cycle problem that trips up so many technology companies. In fact, there may even be a countercyclical element to Computer Associates' business. Because its software makes it possible to squeeze more work out of computers, the need for it is most critical when new hardware purchases are being cut back. This was probably an important factor in allowing the company to grow very nicely right through the technology slump of 1984–1986, when 9 companies out of 10 seemed to be posting disappointing earnings.

Another very important contributor to Computer Associates' consistency has been its base of recurring revenue. The standard software industry practice is to license products on a perpetual basis—the customer pays a one-time fee, which entitles him to use the software for as long as he wants. This is usually the software company's only revenue, except for an annual maintenance fee, which most users pay to get revisions and updates to the program. However, in contrast to the standard practice, Computer Associates offers many of its products under lower priced 3-year licenses. Renewal of these licenses is all but automatic.

By following this strategy, Computer Associates sacrifices some money upfront, but in return it continues to collect revenue for as long as the customers use the product. This stream of recurring revenue, which accounts for about 30% of the company's total sales, is very important. It helps to dampen a lot of the volatility that is caused by normal fluctuations in the signing of new business. And most important, it gives management a measure of visibility that makes it much easier to plan and operate the business.

A final factor that has helped Computer Associates to grow rapidly is its strong financial position. The company has always earned a very respectable return on its shareholders' equity and has avoided carrying much debt on its balance sheet. It has been able to do this because its business isn't very capital-intensive. Once a software company has devel-

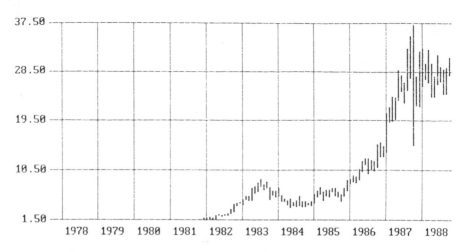

Figure 1.2. Computer Associates International stock chart. Courtesy of Bridge Information Systems, Inc.

oped a program, all it has to do is duplicate it onto disks or tape. There is no real manufacturing involved. So, unlike a chemical company or an automobile manufacturer, Computer Associates doesn't have to make expensive investments in plant or inventory. This has enabled it to finance much of its growth with retained earnings. From time to time, the company has made secondary stock offerings to raise additional funds but always on terms that have been quite favorable. So dilution from an increased number of shares outstanding has never been much of a drag on its rate of growth.

All of these favorable characteristics—a fertile business environment, a well-conceived and well-executed strategy, and the ability to self-finance a lot of its growth—combined with a strong management team have enabled Computer Associates to achieve its enviable record. And as you can see from the stock chart (Figure 1.2), long-term shareholders have been generously rewarded for this strong growth. Over the 5-year period shown previously, Computer Associates stock provided a compound annual return of more than 60%, in spite of the fact that during much of this time emerging growth stocks, and technology stocks in particular, were out of favor with investors.

Naturally, every emerging growth investor dreams of buying a stock like Computer Associates before it becomes well known by the investment community. Then, as it gradually gains wider recognition, other investors bid up the price until the P/E ratio more accurately reflects the company's future growth potential. The early investor enjoys the full leverage of an expanding multiple applied to a rapidly growing stream of earnings. This is the ultimate promise of the emerging growth style of investing.

But even the investor who was late and bought Computer Associates at what turned out to be too high a multiple of earnings still received a respectable return, if he had the patience to hold the stock long enough for the earnings to eventually carry it higher. For instance, in June 1983 the stock sold at a P/E ratio of $36\times$ that year's earnings. In spite of continued earnings growth, it subsequently declined more than 50% when investor sentiment toward small technology companies turned sour. However, a shareholder who maintained his position through the end of the 1987 fiscal year would still have realized an annual return of more than 30% because continued earnings growth eventually overwhelmed the P/E contraction. *This is the beauty of high growth: If you buy the stock right, your return should at least match the rate at which the company's earnings grow; but if you buy it wrong, the growth will eventually bail you out.*

THE RISKS

The very high returns that are possible with small company stocks like Computer Associates illustrate the promise of emerging growth investing. But these potentially high returns have their price. It takes the form of above-average risk.

Much of this risk comes from the fundamental business characteristics of emerging growth companies, something that is clearly reflected in the turnover that has occurred in *Business Week's* annual list of the 100 "best" small companies. Candidates for this list include all publicly owned companies with annual revenue of less than $150 million. The top 100 are then selected on the basis of a composite score that takes into account their growth of sales and earnings and their return on capital. The 1988 list of 100 companies included only 34 that repeated from the prior year, and the 1987 list had just 31 repeaters. Each year a few were dropped from the list because they were acquired or outgrew the revenue cutoff, but most fell off because their growth and profitability measurements declined.

This helps put Computer Associates' record into perspective. In fact, it's really quite an exceptional company. As you can see from the turnover of the *Business Week* list, it's very common for small companies to encounter fundamental problems and stumble as they attempt to grow into big companies. Many never regain their momentum, and they turn out to be very disappointing investments.

One characteristic that creates a high level of business risk for emerging growth companies is the same lack of diversification that can also be an advantage to them. A tightly focused company is great as long as its product line continues to grow, but, once it stops, there is nothing left to fall back on. This is essentially what happened to Worlds of Wonder, the toy company whose Teddy Ruxpin talking doll enjoyed fabulous popularity for a while. Even though it spent a lot of money and a lot of energy trying to broaden its base, it essentially remained a one-product company, and when that product stopped growing, so did the company. By the time management realized what was going on, the business was completely out of control. Not only did Worlds of Wonder stop growing, it soon declared bankruptcy.

Another risk associated with emerging growth companies is their tendency to attract competition from larger companies who have the financial strength to subsidize losses while they are entering a market and battling for share. A particularly memorable (although not current) example of this was Bowmar Instruments, the company that made the first handheld calculators. For a short time it had the market all to itself, and its growth was spectacular. Then Texas Instruments, Hewlett Packard, and a host of Japanese companies got into the business. Not only were the new entrants much bigger, they also manufactured their own semiconductors. This gave them a significant cost advantage relative to Bowmar, which had to buy its chips from outside suppliers. When the competition heated up, Bowmar quickly slipped out of the picture. Without a defensible market niche, or some proprietary advantage that will keep its larger rivals at bay, it's usually very difficult for a small company like Bowmar to sustain its growth when its market becomes more competitive.

However, the most common risk factor—one that is shared by all emerging growth companies to some degree—is the strain on both organizations and people that inevitably accompanies rapid growth. The faster a company grows, the more obstacles it must contend with—the more new employees it must hire, the more new capacity it must start up and bring onstream, the more new products it must develop, and the more changes it must make in the way it does business. All of these obstacles increase the odds that something will go wrong and that management will not be able to keep the company under control. And when a very fast growing company does go out of control, repairing the damage and setting it back on course is often excruciatingly difficult and time consuming. It's a lot like having a tire go flat while you're driving. If you're in the family station wagon going 30 mph on a quiet street, at worst you will suffer some inconvenience and delay. But if you're in a Porsche going down the autobahn at 145 mph, you can consider yourself lucky if you don't end up in a ball of flame.

When an emerging growth company does disappoint investors with a significant earnings shortfall, the resulting decline in the stock price is usually severe because of market-related risk factors. Primary among these is the fact that emerging growth stocks generally sell at a higher P/E ratio than the overall market. So when investors turn sour on one, it has farther to fall. This is compounded by the fact that dividend yields are typically low or nonexistent. It usually makes sense for emerging growth companies to reinvest most of their earnings in future growth, instead of paying them out. But this policy also deprives the stocks of any yield support. And finally, it's rare for investors to attribute any significant underlying asset value to emerging growth companies, as they often do with larger capitalization companies that own, for example, natural resource reserves, real estate, a brand name, or some other type of business franchise that has obvious value, even in the absence of earnings.

THE EMERGING GROWTH INVESTOR

In spite of its above-average risk, the emerging growth style makes sense for many investors because of its potentially high returns. To consider including it as part of your overall investment program, you should have the following characteristics:

1. A stomach for risk.
2. Financial staying power.
3. The ability to make a sufficient commitment of time and effort.

We've already touched on the basic factors that make emerging growth stocks risky. You should realize that mistakes are very common with this kind of investing. Even the most seasoned veterans make a lot of them because there is so much fundamental business risk in small, rapidly growing companies. You must have the stomach to tolerate this risk and plenty of patience. Otherwise, you won't give the emerging growth style enough time to have a fair chance of working in your favor.

You also need to have a certain amount of financial staying power. Emerging growth stocks sometimes go through cycles of poor performance, and even negative returns, that can be severe and last for several years. So they are no place to park money that you may need in a year or two. You should think in terms of owning at least 10 different stocks to give yourself adequate diversification. This means a minimum investment in the neighborhood of $5,000 to $10,000. If you want to invest less than this amount, you'll probably be better off buying a mutual fund that specializes in emerging growth.

Finally, you have to be willing to devote adequate time and effort to the process. Many individual investors have been soured on emerging growth because they have overlooked this requirement. Rather than considering emerging growth stocks as a separate and distinct part of their overall investment program, they just haphazardly take an occasional flyer on a small company. Typically, it's on the recommendation of their broker, or a friend. Because they haven't done any research on their own, because they usually don't know what to look for anyway, and because they don't have adequate diversification within the emerging growth sector, they get burned more often than not. Eventually, they come to the conclusion that emerging growth companies are just too speculative and risky to bother with. Unfortunately, they may be depriving themselves of high returns because they don't recognize that the problem is more in their sloppy execution than in the philosophy.

MUTUAL FUNDS VERSUS DOING IT YOURSELF

If you think emerging growth stocks are appropriate as part of your overall investment program, but can't devote much time to them, you should give serious thought to a mutual fund that specializes in this sector. With a fund, you're buying professional management, and you can be certain that someone will always be looking out for the stocks in the portfolio. Another advantage of investing through a mutual fund is the diversification you gain. A mutual fund's portfolio will include anywhere from 30 to more than 150 different stocks—a lot more than most individual investors can afford or have the time to follow on their own.

Because of their size and the commission dollars they control, mutual funds have excellent access to information and research. When an influential analyst turns cautious on a stock, you can bet the fund manager who owns 200,000 shares is going to hear about it before the individual investor with 200 shares in his portfolio. But size can also be a serious disadvantage, particularly in the emerging growth sector. To start, most of these stocks are very illiquid. It's usually hard to move large blocks without having a significant impact on price. This is a problem for institutional investors, but not much of one for an individual who is buying or selling no more than a few hundred shares.

The same lack of liquidity can also force a mutual fund to carry too many stocks in its portfolio. Diversification is fine up to a point, but it doesn't take long to reach a level where owning one more name in the portfolio really makes little difference. So individual investors have another important advantage because they can be more selective.

For most investors, the issue of whether to own emerging growth stocks directly or through a mutual fund is not an either/or question. There is no reason not to combine the advantages of both. Besides increasing your diversification, there can be a trading advantage to putting part of your emerging growth assets into a fund. If at some point you decide to reduce your overall exposure to this sector of the market, it's easier and cheaper to do so by trimming back your fund holding because you don't have to worry about commissions or trading in round lots.

The purpose of this book is to help individual investors, who want to own emerging growth stocks directly, to actually realize the high returns that are possible with this style of investing. We'll spend considerable time on stock selection, which I consider the backbone of the entire investment management process. These chapters will help you to recognize the factors that allow some small companies to achieve high growth on a consistent basis and to recognize the stumbling blocks that make so many other small companies prone to earnings shortfalls and disappointing stock performance. They'll help you to tell the difference between a Computer Associates, and a Worlds of Wonder, or a Bowmar. You'll still make mistakes, but you can do a lot to decrease the odds of owning too many dogs.

We'll also talk about other aspects of emerging growth investing—valuation, trading strategies, and when to sell. But first we'll take up a very basic topic: when to play and when not to. Sometimes the thing that's smartest to do and hardest to do is stay on the sidelines.

2

Cycles of Valuation: When to Play and When to Stay on the Sidelines

Emerging growth investing is like a game that's a lot easier to win on certain days than others. Fortunately, however, you don't have to play every day. You have the luxury of waiting until your chance of winning is best. Imagine what an advantage this would be if you were managing a baseball team. Say your ace left-handed pitcher needed to rest his arm. You just wouldn't play until he was strong again. Or maybe your lead-off batter couldn't steal bases because a sore ankle was slowing him down. You would just wait until he had his normal speed back. This is the kind of advantage you have with emerging growth stocks if you know how to pick your spots. Knowing when to play and when not to play is one of the most important things you can do to lower risk and improve the odds that you'll be successful.

Your best chance of winning at emerging growth is when the full impact of strong earnings growth gets translated directly into stock returns. This can happen only if the P/E ratios of emerging growth stocks are stable or expanding. Expanding P/Es are best because they leverage high growth into even higher stock returns.

In this chapter we'll see how cycles of valuation within the emerging growth sector of the market influence the odds of winning. Our starting point is past cycles. The philosopher Santayana observed that those who ignore history are condemned to repeat it. Although he probably didn't have emerging growth investing in mind, his warning is still relevant.

CHOOSING AN INDEX

The first thing any student of stock market history needs is an index—the basic yardstick for measuring how stocks have performed over time. Of course the best known market index is the Dow Jones Industrial Average. The Dow is comprised of just 30 blue chip stocks, so it's narrowly based and not very representative of the overall equity market. But it's the index that everyone from your broker to the evening news broadcaster refers to. Even though the S&P 500 is a better index, the Dow is far more popular for describing market moves. In large part its preeminence is attributable to its long history. Charles Dow, one of the founders of *The Wall Street Journal*, began publishing it over 100 years ago.

Within the emerging growth sector of the market there are several indexes to choose from. Among the brokerage firms, both Hambrecht & Quist and Morgan Stanley maintain indexes that they publish regularly. And many investors consider the NASDAQ Industrial Index a reasonably good proxy. However, the most popular measure of emerging growth performance is the T. Rowe Price New Horizons Fund. New Horizons is the granddaddy of all emerging growth funds, and like the Dow, its big advantage is the length of its record.

New Horizons is an open-end, no load mutual fund that was started in June 1960. From its inception, it has followed a consistent policy of investing only in small, rapidly growing companies across a broad spectrum of consumer, service, and technology industries. It has never attempted to anticipate swings in the market, so changes in its cash position have not had a significant impact on its performance. Because New Horizons is not an unmanaged portfolio like the Dow or the S&P 500, it's actually not an index in the strict sense of the word. However, the consistency of its policy and the length of its record make it the best available proxy for the emerging growth sector of the stock market.

PAST CYCLES

Table 2.1 shows the annual performance of both New Horizons and the S&P 500 for each year since 1961, the fund's first full year of operations. From its inception through the end of 1987, New Horizons' average annual rate of return has been slightly higher than that of the S&P 500. But within this span of years there have been some very significant variations that become apparent when it is divided into cycles of performance. Returns for these cycles are shown in the two right-hand columns of Table 2.1. The length and severity of the down cycles are a sharp reminder that emerging

TABLE 2.1 Performance of New Horizons Fund versus S&P 500

| Year Ending 12/31 | ANNUAL RATE OF TOTAL RETURN | | AVERAGE ANNUAL RATE OF RETURN OVER CYCLE | |
	New Horizons Fund	S&P 500	New Horizons Fund	S&P 500
1961	16.8%	26.9%		
1962	−29.0	−8.7	−1.9%	13.5%
1963	9.7	22.8		
1964	1.8	16.5		
1965	43.7	12.5		
1966	18.5	−10.1		
1967	86.7	24.0		
1968	23.2	11.1	25.2	7.7
1969	−6.8	−8.4		
1970	−11.9	3.9		
1971	54.0	14.3		
1972	21.7	19.0		
1973	−41.9	−14.7		
1974	−38.7	−26.5	−13.8	1.6
1975	39.6	37.2		
1976	11.1	23.9		
1977	12.7	−7.1		
1978	20.8	6.6		
1979	35.5	18.6	22.0	10.2
1980	57.6	32.4		
1981	−7.8	−5.0		
1982	22.8	21.6		
1983	19.5	22.6		
1984	−9.6	6.2		
1985	24.3	31.7	4.5	16.5
1986	−0.2	18.7		
1987	−7.2	5.3		

SOURCE: T. Rowe Price Associates, Inc.

growth investing is risky—even beyond the fundamental business characteristics of the companies themselves. If you buy emerging growth stocks at the peak of their popularity, as so many investors do, you'll have a hard time earning a competitive return, no matter how fast the portfolio companies' earnings grow.

New Horizons itself began at one of these times, and as a result, its start was anything but auspicious. During the 1961–1964 period, the fund's net asset value declined slightly, whereas the S&P 500 was providing an annual return of 13.5%. Because of its lagging performance, some dissatisfied shareholders suggested that "New Horizontal" would have been a more apt name for the fund. But this early period of underperformance created valuation levels that set the stage for the powerful up cycle that began in 1965 and continued all the way through 1972. In spite of 2 down years in 1969 and 1970, New Horizons yielded an outstanding 25.2% annual return over this period, versus 7.7% for the S&P 500. During these years, expanding P/E ratios leveraged the underlying earnings growth of the portfolio companies into even higher stock returns. It was truly a golden era for growth stock investing, and New Horizons represented this style taken to its extreme. Never has there been a better time to play the emerging growth game.

New Horizons' strong performance over these years won it a great deal of publicity and enormous popularity with investors. By 1972, when the cycle was about to reach its end, money was pouring in faster than it could be invested, and the fund was actually forced to stop accepting new subscriptions. However, it remained so popular that for a while some brokers maintained an over-the-counter market in its shares. Investors who were unfortunate enough to have bought New Horizons this way got clobbered two ways. Besides paying the highest prices, they were also saddled with brokerage commissions that they wouldn't have incurred a few years later when the fund was again open to new subscriptions and selling at about one third of its peak value.

This peak in popularity was immediately followed by the sharpest correction in the fund's history. During 1973 and 1974, New Horizons plummeted a breathtaking 65%. A lot of shell-shocked investors felt as if they were reliving 1929 in a slow motion.

Of course, New Horizons' drop was largely attributable to a vicious bear market that ripped all stocks in those years. A major cause of the overall market decline was the oil crisis, which brought about soaring inflation and sharply higher interest rates as well as serious concerns about the international banking system's ability to cope with the massive sums of wealth that were suddenly being transferred from the industrial nations to Middle East oil producers. These shocks soon led to a recession. And if this was not enough to shatter confidence by itself, there was also the Watergate crisis to worry about. On top of which, emerging growth investors—the few who were still left—had yet another cross to bear in the form of ERISA, the Employee Retirement Income Security Act. This legislation, designed to protect the beneficiaries of employee pension plans, created some doubt as to whether it was even appropriate for pension funds to invest in the emerging growth sector. Although this concern eventually faded and emerging growth stocks were accepted as suitable investments, the initial doubt certainly depressed their valuation.

The combination of all these negative factors accounted for New Horizons' severe decline in 1973 and 1974. In 1975 the fund recovered slightly more than the S&P 500, but in 1976 it again lagged the overall market by a considerable margin. Over the 4-year cycle, New Horizons declined by an average of 13.8% annually, compared to a slightly positive total return of 1.6% for the S&P 500. (The price of the S&P 500 actually fell slightly over these 4 years, but its dividend yield was high enough to push its total return into plus territory.)

It's noteworthy that during the 1973–1976 period, in spite of the turbulent economic environment, the New Horizons' portfolio companies as a whole maintained positive earnings growth. The fund's negative return wasn't caused by a lack of earnings growth but rather was the result of severe multiple contraction. As shown in Figure 2.1, New Horizons sold at a P/E of nearly 35× forward earnings during 1972. By the end of 1974, its multiple had dropped to under 10×. There was simply no way that earnings growth could offset such severe multiple contraction in so short a period of time.

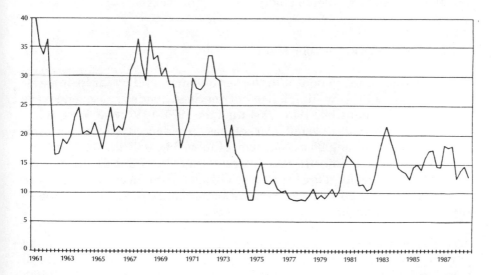

Figure 2.1. T. Rowe Price New Horizons Fund P/E ratio of fund's portfolio securities (12 months forward). This chart is intended to show the history of the average (unweighted) P/E ratio of the fund's portfolio companies. Earnings per share are estimated by the fund's investment advisor from each quarter end. Courtesy of T. Rowe Price Associates, Inc.

Of course, the overall market also saw a sharp drop in P/E ratios during this period. It was caused by the extraordinary rise in inflation and interest rates. Investors didn't feel very confident about the future, and if money market funds were offering returns well into double digits, it was hard to see any reason to pay a high multiple for uncertain earnings. This change in psychology had a particularly devastating effect on emerging growth stocks. In 1972 New Horizons' multiple was about twice as high as the market's multiple; by the end of 1976 it had lost virtually all of this premium.

The severe multiple contraction that took place over these years drove New Horizons down to about the same level of relative valuation that prevailed in early 1965, when it had begun its last cycle of strong performance. And just as had happened in that earlier period, by the end of 1976 emerging growth stocks were again poised to outperform the general market by a wide margin. By this point, the risk of further multiple contraction had been washed out, and New Horizons was in a position to enjoy the full benefit of the portfolio companies' earnings growth. As a result, the fund registered a compound annual return of 22.0% over the 6-year period of 1977–1982; this compared to 10.2% for the S&P 500. The relative performance didn't quite match that of the earlier 1965–1972 up cycle, but it was still an excellent time to own emerging growth stocks.

RECENT UNDERPERFORMANCE

New Horizons' third period of underperformance, and by far its longest, began in 1983. At this writing it has not yet clearly ended. In several ways this cycle is a lot more like 1961–1964 than the 1973–1976 cycle. First, it has taken place while the overall market has experienced strong performance—notwithstanding Black Monday, October 19, 1987, the day the Dow fell more than 500 points. It's also different from the 1973–1976 down cycle in that the reasons for it are much less obvious. A number of causes have clearly contributed to the poor relative performance of emerging growth stocks, but it's difficult to say which of them has been most important.

Certainly one factor has been the massive restructuring of oil and other basic industry companies in the form of mergers, spinoffs, and leveraged buy-outs. These financial maneuverings have raised the stock prices of many of the large, asset-rich companies that comprise most of the S&P 500, but they've had a negligible impact on the emerging growth sector. Similarly, the declining value of the dollar has been a much greater benefit to large multinationals than to emerging growth companies, many of which don't even have meaningful overseas operations.

Recent years have also witnessed a massive inflow of foreign investment to the U.S. stock market, but it has been directed almost exclusively into large capitalization companies, rather than emerging growth companies. And yet another factor that has penalized the relative performance of emerging growth stocks has been the continuing popularity of indexing on the part of institutions. Instead of trying to beat the market, many pension funds have opted to invest in a package of stocks designed to duplicate the performance of the S&P 500. This has naturally contributed to the flow of money into the index stocks, few of which are emerging growth companies. At the same time, a proliferation of new instruments like index options and stock futures have become available for speculative money that might otherwise have flowed into emerging growth investments. So many of the trends that have had the strongest influence on stock prices during these years have either bypassed the emerging growth sector or have actually worked against it.

However, what may have been the most important reason of all for New Horizons' relative underperformance was the collapse of small technology stocks that began in the second half of 1983. Although the annual returns shown in Table 2.1 indicate that New Horizons' performance was quite close to that of the S&P 500 in 1982 and 1983, there were actually very large variances on a quarterly basis. During the last half of 1982 and the first half of 1983, New Horizons outperformed the market by a wide margin. Most of the excess return was attributable to its large holding of technology stocks, which had extraordinarily good performance during these four quarters.

In late 1982, investment bankers and venture capitalists recognized that a new bull market was underway and, taking advantage of this opportunity, they lined up all kinds of small technology companies for initial public offerings. Many of these companies had been started only a year or two earlier and never should have been brought out, but by mid-1983 there was a flood of offerings underway. And investors were willing to snap up almost anything because practically all of the earlier deals had done so well. It was a time when greed overwhelmed fear as the dominant emotion of the day. The unfortunate result was unsustainable prices for a lot of low quality companies that never had much chance of delivering the earnings their investment bankers promised.

The inevitable correction started in the second half of 1983, when a number of technology companies began to encounter slowing demand. Up until then, it seemed that every large corporation in the world had been on a buying spree for high-tech capital equipment. Now it was suddenly time for them to step back, assess what they had bought, and figure out how to use it. The sudden slowdown in demand caught a lot of the unsea-

soned companies off guard and caused numerous earnings disappointments. These were exacerbated by estimates that had been overly optimistic, and by valuations that had been excessive. The result was a severe
correction in small technology stocks across the board. Even companies
whose earnings continued to grow were not immune to it. For example,
Digital Communications Associates stock fell 44% in the 12 months ending
June 1984—even though the company's earnings more than doubled during the same period. It's frightening to think what might have happened if
the earnings had been disappointing.

Although investor disenchantment with small growth companies was
focused primarily on technology stocks, it was so severe that it had a spill-
over effect on other sectors of the emerging growth market. This was probably the most important reason for New Horizons' relative underperformance during these years.

THE RELATIVE P/E RATIO

Many investors automatically equate emerging growth stocks with high
beta stocks. Beta is a statistic developed and popularized by academics to
relate the return on a single stock or a portfolio to the return on the overall
market. Theoretically, a stock or portfolio with a high beta should outperform a rising market and underperform a falling market. New Horizons
has had a tendency to do this on average, but the correlation of its returns
to the overall market is surprisingly weak. For instance, in 1986 the fund
was down marginally, whereas the S&P posted a very healthy 18.7% return. Even if you had somehow known ahead of time exactly what kind of
year the market was going to have, this knowledge wouldn't have helped
at all in predicting the performance of emerging growth stocks.

A better indicator of the emerging growth sector's potential for outper-
forming the overall market is a measure known as the New Horizons' relative P/E. This is simply the ratio of New Horizons' P/E to that of the S&P
500, calculated on estimated 12-month forward earnings for both the fund
and the S&P. Shown here in Figure 2.2, it is published periodically in New
Horizons' quarterly reports to shareholders, and by Morgan Stanley.

As you might expect, the five cycles of relative performance shown in
Table 2.1 have been strongly influenced by changes in New Horizons' relative P/E. Each of the three down cycles started with the relative P/E at or
very close to 2.0×, meaning that the fund's P/E was about double that of
the S&P 500. These down cycles didn't play themselves out until the fund's
relative P/E had declined to nearly 1.0× the S&P 500, wiping out almost
all of the valuation premium that existed at the peak. During these down

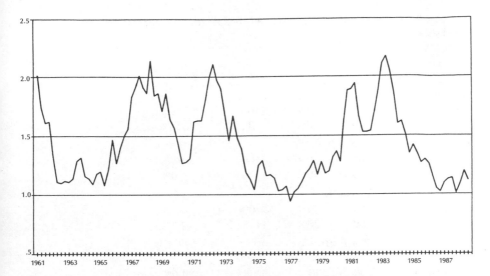

Figure 2.2. T. Rowe Price New Horizons Fund P/E ratio of the fund's portfolio securities relative to the S&P 500 P/E ratio (12 months forward). This chart is intended to show the history of the average (unweighted) P/E ratio of the fund's portfolio companies compared with the P/E Ratio of the S&P 500 Index. Earnings per share are estimated by the fund's investment advisor from each quarter end. Courtesy of T. Rowe Price Associates, Inc.

cycles severe multiple contraction offset the superior earnings growth of the fund's portfolio companies. These were times when it was best to watch the action from the sidelines, as one player after another was carried off on a stretcher.

Conversely, periods of relative multiple expansion—like the one from 1977 through 1982—are the times when you want to own emerging growth stocks. During these up cycles, strong earnings growth is compounded by multiple expansion to produce very high returns.

Table 2.2 illustrates the profound impact that changes in the relative P/E can have on performance over a 4-year period. In this hypothetical example, the S&P 500 is assumed to experience annual earnings growth of 7%. Its P/E stays constant at 10x, so capital appreciation is exactly equal to the 7% rate of earnings growth. A dividend yield of 4% brings the S&P's total return up to 11%. The emerging growth portfolio is assumed to have annual earnings growth of 20% and no dividend yield.

In Case I the relative multiple declines from 2.0x to 1.0x. This contraction almost totally obliterates the earnings growth, leaving only a meager 1% annual return. In Case II the multiple assumption is reversed, with the relative P/E expanding from 1.0x to 2.0x. The expanding multiple leverages the 20% earnings growth up to an annual return of nearly 43%.

TABLE 2.2 How Changes in the Relative Multiple Affect Emerging Growth Stocks' Performance

	Earnings	P/E	Price	Appreciation	Yield	Total Return
Market (S&P 500)						
Today	$10.00	10×	$100			
4 Years	$13.10	10×	$131	7.0%	4.0%	11.0%
Emerging Growth (Case I)						
Today	$5.00	20×	$100			
4 Years	$10.40	10×	$104	1.0%	—	1.0%
Emerging Growth (Case II)						
Today	$10.00	10×	$100			
4 Years	$20.80	20×	$416	42.8%	—	42.8%
Emerging Growth (Case III)						
Today	$10.00	10×	$100			
4 Years	$20.80	10×	$208	20.0%	—	20.0%

If you had invested $10,000 under Case I, at the end of 4 years it would have been worth only about $10,400. You wouldn't have actually lost money, but you would have done better with a money market fund, and your return certainly wouldn't have been high enough to justify the risk. But under Case II the same $10,000 initial investment would have been worth more than $41,000 after 4 years, and your opinion of emerging growth investing would have been considerably more favorable. Such a wide variation in results may seem unrealistically extreme, but the underlying assumptions do have historic precedent in the actual behavior of the New Horizons Fund.

A BAROMETER OF EMERGING GROWTH VALUE

Historically, the New Horizons' relative P/E has been an excellent indicator of whether or not to play the emerging growth game. Whenever it has been at a level of 1.15× or lower, it has been relatively easy to make money with emerging growth stocks. At these points, they have been valued at a premium of no more than 15% to the overall market—a level at which investors are willing to pay very little for future growth. Sometimes there is a hint of recession in the air, and it seems safer to own defensive stocks like food companies or utilities, whose earnings usually show little sensitivity to the economic environment. Sometimes inflation is the worry of the day, and asset-rich companies or cyclicals with good pricing flexibility look like superior vehicles for providing a return higher than the inflation rate. However, these phases of negative investor psychology have always blown over.

Over New Horizons' history there have been 18 quarters when it has sold at a relative P/E of 1.15× or lower. Results for the subsequent 3-year periods are shown in Table 2.3. In all but 4 of these 18 periods, New Horizons outperformed the S&P. At worst, its compound annual return was 8.9%, and on average it was 25.3%. Similar data for 5-year periods are shown in Table 2.4. If anything, these results are even more impressive. New Horizons' return was higher than the S&P in all 18 of these 5-year periods.

TABLE 2.3 New Horizons Fund: Average Performance Following Periods of Low Relative P/E Ratios

| | | 3-YEAR PERFORMANCE | |
Quarter	Relative P/E	NHF	S&P 500
2Q '62	1.11	+ 29.2%	+69.2%
3Q '62	1.10	+ 43.7	+75.8
4Q '62	1.12	+ 60.6	+64.4
1Q '63	1.11	+ 64.3	+47.1
2Q '63	1.14	+ 65.4	+36.2
2Q '64	1.14	+161.4	+22.2
3Q '64	1.09	+198.7	+26.6
2Q '65	1.08	+239.9	+30.5
3Q '74	1.13	+ 71.8	+72.9
4Q '74	1.04	+ 74.8	+57.9
1Q '76	1.14	+ 43.5	+14.3
2Q '76	1.03	+ 53.6	+14.6
3Q '76	1.04	+ 75.4	+21.0
4Q '76	1.07	+ 84.6	+17.4
1Q '77	0.94	+ 79.0	+21.6
2Q '77	1.02	+ 94.8	+33.6
3Q '77	1.05	+142.3	+52.8
4Q '77	1.11	+158.1	+67.5
	High	+239.9%	+75.8%
	Low	+ 29.2	+14.3
	Mean	+ 96.7	+41.4
	Median	+ 75.1	+33.6
No. Periods NHF Outperformed S&P 500: 14 out of 18			

SOURCE: T. Rowe Price Associates, Inc.

TABLE 2.4 New Horizons Fund: Average Performance Following Periods of Low Relative P/E Ratios

| Quarter | Relative P/E | 5-YEAR PERFORMANCE | |
		NHF	S&P 500
2Q '62	1.11	+211.0%	+ 94.8%
3Q '62	1.10	+241.8	+101.9
4Q '62	1.12	+255.2	+ 79.3
1Q '63	1.11	+209.7	+ 58.9
2Q '63	1.14	+274.5	+ 51.2
2Q '64	1.14	+261.1	+ 40.2
3Q '64	1.09	+254.8	+ 11.0
2Q '65	1.08	+134.9	− 5.5
3Q '74	1.13	+178.3	+118.1
4Q '74	1.04	+186.3	+ 99.7
1Q '76	1.14	+187.7	+ 69.9
2Q '76	1.03	+200.4	+ 62.1
3Q '76	1.04	+154.6	+ 42.7
4Q '76	1.07	+168.1	+ 47.8
1Q '77	0.94	+153.5	+ 48.0
2Q '77	1.02	+126.7	+ 42.5
3Q '77	1.05	+147.7	+ 63.4
4Q '77	1.11	+192.1	+ 93.5
	High	+274.5%	+118.1%
	Low	+126.7	− 5.5
	Mean	+196.6	+ 62.2
	Median	+189.9	+ 58.9
No. Periods NHF Outperformed S&P 500: 18 out of 18			

SOURCE: T. Rowe Price Associates, Inc.

Some emerging growth investors object to using the New Horizons' relative P/E as a valuation tool because it is based on estimates of future earnings. They point out that even in the unlikely event that the New Horizons' analysts make conservative estimates, there is still no allowance for companies that stumble badly and experience severe earnings short- falls. This produces a strong tendency for the New Horizons' earnings estimates to be inflated, and consequently for its P/E to be understated.

The critics' observation is valid but probably makes little difference. As long as the relative P/E is understated on a reasonably consistent basis, it's still a useful tool for gauging the attractiveness of the emerging growth sector relative to other stocks. And because the fund has steadily held to its original philosophy and has had good continuity of management, its biases very likely have been consistent. In other words, it may be slightly flawed, but it's still the best tool available. If you're trying to navigate a ship through stormy waters, a compass that's a few degrees off is better than none at all.

WILL IT CONTINUE TO WORK?

On the basis of the historical data shown in Tables 2.3 and 2.4, it's tempting to conclude that the New Horizons' relative P/E is a very useful valuation tool. The only problem is that the most recent measurement period began more than a decade ago. The world has undergone tremendous changes since then, not the least of which have occurred in financial markets. So we ought to ask ourselves whether the old valuation ranges still hold. Or, like a river succumbing to powerful geologic forces, has New Horizons' channel been permanently shifted by events of the last decade?

On the low side at least, it seems likely that no change has occurred. There's good reason to believe a relative P/E of around 1.0x will continue to delineate the bottom of New Horizons' relative valuation range. To see why, let's look at Case III in Table 2.2. Under this scenario, the relative P/E remains constant at 1.0x throughout the entire period. Because the emerging growth companies' earnings compound at a 20% rate, the portfolio also has a 20% annual rate of return—9% higher than the S&P's return. And as long as the relative P/E remains at 1.0x, this superior return is available for no premium whatever. But this is too much of a bargain to last very long. Eventually investors will develop enough confidence to pay some premium for the higher return, and, in the process, they will bid the emerging growth P/E to a level above that of the overall market. So it's easy to conclude that emerging growth stocks should sell at some premium to the market.

It's much more difficult to say how much of a premium is fair, and how much is excessive. A theoretically correct valuation model would take into account factors such as growth rates, sustainability of growth, eventual dividend payouts, and rates of return available from Treasury Bills and other investment alternatives. But I seriously doubt that this approach, even though theoretically superior, is really any more useful than simply accepting history as a guide. On this basis, relative multiples of 1.5–1.6x should continue to represent fair value. And again, there are bound to be periods when emerging growth gets so popular that enthusiastic investors drive the relative P/E above 2.0. Just as in the past, these valuation levels will be excessive, and it will be time to cut your exposure close to zero.

WHY IT'S HARD TO USE

Because it's quite reasonable to expect the New Horizons' relative P/E to continue fluctuating between its historic extremes, you should be able to use it confidently for gauging the attractiveness of emerging growth stocks and adjust your portfolio accordingly. The obvious strategy is to shift between stocks and cash, according to the reading provided by the relative P/E. Below 1.15×, you hold almost no cash and maximize your exposure to stocks. But you gradually cut back as the relative P/E rises. By the time it reaches 2.0×, you've reduced stocks to a minimum and hold plenty of cash.

As straightforward and simple as this strategy seems, it's incredibly difficult to implement effectively. The problem is that human emotions inevitably get in the way. The relative multiple always reaches excessive levels at the very same time that investors have just experienced several years of excellent relative performance. And their recent success always fosters a feeling of great confidence. Naturally most investors attribute their good results to superior insights and excellence in stock picking. They tend to down play the role of relative P/E expansion, if they even acknowledge it at all. Changes in the relative P/E are always trotted out as an excuse for poor performance but are very seldom mentioned as a reason for good results.

And when periods of peak valuation occur, there are usually plenty of rationalizations floating around to reinforce investors' confidence. For instance, in mid-1983, with the relative P/E in record high territory, at least one reputable analyst published a valuation model showing his list of emerging growth stocks to still be well below their intrinsic value. At the same time, other "experts" were arguing that the underlying growth rate of the New Horizons companies was higher than it had ever been in the past and therefore the old valuation guidelines were too low.

Almost by definition, the emotional commitment to emerging growth stocks is the strongest just at the time when the sector reaches its most dangerous point of overvaluation. Remember how in 1972, with the relative P/E at 2.0×, New Horizons had to stop accepting new subscriptions because the money was coming in so fast. Three years later, when emerging growth stocks sold at almost no premium to the market, the fund's problem was redemptions rather than subscriptions.

The flip side of the valuation coin is that the most attractive opportunities for investing in emerging growth occur precisely when negative sentiment is the strongest. Just as overvaluation always follows a period of strong relative performance, undervaluation is always preceded by several years of poor performance. At this point, confidence has eroded, investors have lost heart, and pessimism abounds. And this negativism is always reinforced with plausible arguments as to why past benchmarks are no longer valid and future valuation levels will be lower.

During the mid-1970s, the most popular negative scenario was based on the fear that small companies would be denied access to capital at reasonable costs and therefore wouldn't be able to finance high rates of growth. More recently it has been argued that the pace of change in technology has become so rapid that small technology companies, which certainly make up much of the emerging growth universe, should sell at lower than normal P/Es because of this risk. And when the Tax Reform Act of 1986 was passed, the conventional wisdom was that it tipped the scales in favor of mature dividend-paying companies, relative to emerging growth, because it increased the aftertax value of dividends but decreased the value of capital gains. If the relative P/E had been around 2.0x at the time, the prevailing view probably would have been that the legislation favored emerging growth companies because elimination of the investment tax credit had much less impact on them than on more mature companies.

A wise investor once observed the most costly words in the English language are "it's going to be different this time." It's always easy to convince yourself this cycle really is different. To avoid being trapped by this kind of thinking, you have to detach yourself from your emotions and not get carried away with trendy arguments. One way to do this is to make sure you never forget the lessons of history. It can make a huge difference in your investment results.

Part II
Selecting Stocks and Constructing Your Portfolio

3

Basic Stock Selection Standards

Once you've decided the time is right to become an emerging growth player, you have to select the stocks that will make up your portfolio. This is really the backbone of the entire process, for no matter how appealing the emerging growth style of investing may seem in theory, it simply cannot work in practice unless most of your stocks actually deliver earnings growth substantially higher than that of the overall market. Without this growth you have no more chance of succeeding than a singer who can't carry a tune or a pitcher who can't get the ball over the plate. This may seem obvious, but it is so important that it cannot be overemphasized.

This chapter will explain some basic standards that will help you pick stocks that have the best chance of delivering the earnings growth you need. As we have seen in the case of Computer Associates, good stock selection will eventually overcome errors in timing and valuation. So to be really successful, it's important to find companies that can grow on a *sustained* basis. The emerging growth universe is littered with the cold hulks of shooting stars—companies that grew spectacularly for a few years and then burned out. Therefore, the important question isn't how fast a company can grow, but how long it can grow fast.

Stock selection is the one area where individual investors potentially have a tremendous advantage relative to institutions. Because adequate portfolio diversification doesn't require owning more than 10 or 15 well-chosen stocks, individual investors can afford to be very choosy. But institutional investors are denied this luxury because of their size. Some emerging growth mutual funds, for instance, own close to 200 different stocks. It's not because they want to own such a large number or even think they can do a reasonably good job of following this many. Rather, their size forces them to.

Unfortunately, most individual investors forfeit their advantage by taking a casual, *ad hoc* approach to stock selection that is essentially passive. If their broker or a friend suggests a stock idea that sounds reasonable, they buy it. They don't bother to really study the company or compare it to the alternatives. It's very easy to slip into this approach, but you really handicap yourself if you do.

The first rule of stock selection is simply this: Be selective. Think of your portfolio as an Ivy League college, and yourself as the director of admissions. The hardest part about these schools is getting into them in the first place. Because they're able to select their students from so many highly qualified applicants, they can be confident that everyone they admit will have both the motivation and ability to complete their courses successfully. So if the slightest thing about a candidate strikes the director of admissions the wrong way—even if he can't put his finger on it—he will reject that candidate. Unless you're managing a huge portfolio, you enjoy a similar advantage. From the hundreds of attractive candidates available, you need to admit only a handful, so you can be very picky.

In making his selections, the director of admissions doesn't act on every application as it comes across his desk. If he did, he would risk having to turn down some very strong applicants because he had already filled the class. Or, he might accept too many French majors and not enough physics students. To get the strongest class with the best balance, he evaluates each applicant relative to the alternatives. There will be some obvious acceptances and some obvious rejections, but most decisions will require a bit of time and careful consideration. This is the same approach you should take in selecting the stocks that will fill out your portfolio.

DEFINING THE UNIVERSE

The first step in stock selection is just identifying the companies that make up the emerging growth universe. This isn't much of a problem for institutional investors, who are usually inundated with research material. For individual investors, it requires a little more time and effort. An excellent starting place is the business press. *Forbes, Business Week,* and *Inc.* all publish annual cover-story issues on emerging growth stocks that are very helpful. *The Wall Street Journal* and *Investors Daily* will also trigger suggestions from time to time. And more specialized publications like *OTC Review* and *Barron's* are useful. All of these, except *OTC Review,* are probably available at your library.

Somewhat more expensive but also more focused on this sector of the market are the emerging growth stock services published by both Standard & Poor's and Value Line. These come in research format and contain plenty of statistics and factual information as well as specific recommendations. Before you take out your own subscription to these services, check with your broker. He probably has access to them and can lend you a copy.

The quarterly and annual reports of the numerous mutual funds that specialize in emerging growth stocks are another good place to look for candidates. (*Business Week* and *Forbes* both do annual mutual fund issues that will help you identify them.)

Of course, brokers can also be a valuable source of ideas. Although some brokerage firms pay little or no attention to this sector of the market, others are attracted to it because emerging growth companies usually have enormous appetites for capital and therefore make very good investment-banking clients. Brokers also like emerging growth stocks because most of them are traded over the counter, where spreads are normally higher than the commissions on listed stocks. Some of the nationally recognized firms that have made a serious commitment to the emerging growth sector include Morgan Stanley, Robertson Colman, Hambrecht & Quist, and Alex. Brown. And not to be overlooked are the smaller regional firms, who often become aware of promising local companies before they gain broad recognition.

It is important to keep in mind that brokers are invariably much better at recommending stocks to buy than to sell. This is especially true when there is an investment-banking relationship that might be jeopardized if the broker expressed anything other than a positive opinion on the client company's stock. Nevertheless, there are advantages to keeping an account with at least one firm that is a factor in this sector of the market. In addition to providing recommendations and research coverage, they are usually market makers in the over-the-counter stocks their analysts follow and therefore are able to provide better trading execution in them. These brokers also underwrite many of the initial public offerings of promising new issues and control their distribution.

Once you've identified a company that appears to be worth considering as a candidate, gather as much information about it as you can. Write or call the company for annual reports and quarterlies. And ask for the 10-k, a form similar to an annual report that all public companies are required to file with the Securities and Exchange Commission. Occasionally it will contain extra tidbits of information that can be helpful in analyzing a company. Also, ask to be put on the mailing list and request an information package. A lot of companies will send you reprints of articles and analysts' research reports that can be very useful. Finally, see if your broker can also furnish some research.

APPLYING THE BASIC STANDARDS

A good, long list of companies, like the one furnished in the appendix of this book, is important to have as a starting point for stock selection. But by itself, a list is worth very little as an investment tool because it has no predictive value. What you really need is a way of sorting out the small number of exceptional companies that have the best chance of sustaining their growth. This is critical because so many emerging growth companies encounter fundamental problems and then turn out to be poor stock market performers because of their disappointing earnings.

The best way to begin the sorting-out process is by applying a number of basic selection standards to each company on your list of candidates. Many successful emerging growth investors use the following four tests as an integral part of this effort:

1. The past record of growth and profitability.
2. The business environment—Is it conducive to growth?
3. Competition.
4. Management.

Again, think of yourself as the director of admissions. There are many more candidates for your portfolio than you can admit, so you need a way of reducing the number to a managable size from which you can make your final decisions. The basic standards are your way of doing this. The first one, the company's past record of growth and profitability, is a lot like college board scores; it is quantitative and objective. The other standards are more like the college applicant's teacher recommendations, extracurricular activities, and interview. Although a little more subjective, they are very important, nonetheless.

PAST GROWTH AND PROFITABILITY

Be sure to study every candidate's financial statements for the last 3 to 5 years and then answer the following questions:

1. How fast has the company grown?
2. How consistent has it growth been?
3. How profitable is it?
4. How much debt does it carry on its balance sheet?

Although it's not a guarantee by any means, a company that has grown rapidly in the past often has a good chance of continuing to in the future. In evaluating past growth, it's just as important to look at sales as earnings. Some companies are able to show high earnings growth for a while because of margin expansion. There is nothing wrong with this, but it cannot continue indefinitely. I suggest you drop any company whose sales and earnings have not grown at a minimum rate of 20% on average. This cutoff will still leave you with plenty of candidates to look at.

Also check for consistency. If a company's earnings have bounced all around, there is a good chance it's in a cyclical business or a highly competitive one. Businesses like these are tough to control and are prone to disappointing earnings. And in addition to these fundamental considerations, timing the purchase and sale of this kind of stock is always tricky. So you are best off bypassing any company that has had 2 or more down years in the last 5.

Another important criterion to consider is profitability, because it determines how much growth can be financed internally. Most high-growth businesses require a lot of investment. New plants must be built; new products have to be either developed internally or acquired; new employees must be recruited and trained. And often new channels of distribution have to be developed. All of these things are expensive and require financing. The more profitable a company is, the more earnings it will have to plough back into financing these expenditures. Only occasionally will it have to raise additional money by issuing more stock. And when it does turn to the equity markets for financing, it will have the luxury of picking its spots, so the dilution to existing shareholders will be minimal. The best measure of profitability is return on average equity. I recommend you skip any company that does not have a return on average equity of at least 13%.

Finally, it's a good idea to be apprehensive of companies with a lot of debt on their balance sheet. Because they must make interest and principal payments, not all of their cash flow can be reinvested in future growth. Debt also magnifies fluctuations in operating profitability and adds an element of financial risk. And, of course, the fundamental business risk of most emerging growth companies is already high. So it is wise to avoid companies whose debt represents more than 30% of their total capital (debt + equity).

TABLE 3.1 Quantitative Standards

Year	1	2	3	4	5
Company A					
Sales	$18.2	$21.3	$24.1	$28.4	$32.9
Percentage Change	19%	17%	13%	18%	16%
Net Income	1.9	2.2	2.0	2.8	3.3
Earnings Per Share (EPS)	.95	1.09	.98	1.35	1.61
Percentage Change	20%	15%	−10%	38%	19%
Debt	1.4	1.5	1.5	1.8	2.5
Equity	10.6	12.6	14.4	17.0	20.0
Debt/Total Capital	12%	11%	9%	10%	11%
Return on Average Equity	20%	19%	15%	18%	18%
Company B					
Sales	$13.7	$18.6	$23.8	$31.7	$40.3
Percentage Change	42%	36%	28%	33%	27%
Net Income	.8	1.1	1.4	1.8	2.3
EPS	.22	.29	.37	.38	.47
Percentage Change	40%	32%	28%	3%	24%
Debt	2.0	4.5	7.1	5.4	10.0
Equity	8.7	9.8	11.2	19.0	21.3
Debt/Total Capital	19%	31%	39%	22%	32%
Return on Average Equity	10%	12%	13%	12%	11%
Company C					
Sales	$23.8	$31.7	$40.9	$50.7	$63.9
Percentage Change	43%	33%	29%	24%	26%
Net Income	1.3	2.0	3.0	4.2	5.1
EPS	.18	.24	.35	.49	.60
Percentage Change	100% +	33%	46%	40%	22%
Debt	.8	0.0	3.0	2.8	2.6
Equity	2.4	11.4	14.3	18.6	24.0
Debt/Total Capital	25%	0%	17%	13%	10%
Return on Average Equity	76%	29%	23%	26%	24%

Table 3.1 demonstrates the application of these quantitative tests to three different companies. Most of the data shown here can be taken directly from annual reports or S & P sheets. The only numbers that have to be calculated are the percentage changes, the ratio of debt to total capital, and the return on average equity. (The latter is simply net income divided by the average of beginning and ending equity.)

All three of these companies have very respectable financial records, but only Company C passes all the tests. Company A has good profitability and a fairly strong balance sheet, with debt accounting for only about

10% of its total capital on average. Its record has also been quite consistent, with only 1 year of down earnings. Even then the decline was not severe, and it was immediately followed by a good recovery. However, Company A's sales growth is quite unimpressive. You should have little difficulty finding candidates with higher sales growth whose statistics are just as strong in the other categories.

Company B has had much better growth of both sales and earnings and has been quite consistent, too. But its profitability and balance sheet are a little weak. At the end of Year 3, debt had risen to 39% of total capital, and early in the following year the company had to sell stock to bring the ratio down to a more comfortable level. As a result of the dilution, it had only a nominal earnings gain that year. And then by the end of the following year, the debt ratio was up over 30% again. This company's basic problem is that its profitability isn't high enough to finance its growth. Even though it ploughs all of its earnings back into the business, this is not enough; it must also rely heavily on outside sources of capital, either in the form of additional equity or more debt.

Company C does well in all four categories—its sales and earnings have both grown consistently at rates above 20%, its return on equity has been high, and its use of debt financing minimal. Company C is actually Paychex, a company that we'll discuss in a later chapter.

From time to time, you may want to override these tests of past growth and profitability, just as the director of admissions might relax his college board standards slightly to keep the football coach happy. For instance, you might consider making an exception with Company A if you expect its sales growth to pick up because of an upturn in its industry. But you should always have a good reason for making an exception. Otherwise, the standards will lose their effectiveness. Too many mediocre companies will creep into your portfolio, and you will have forfeited your selectivity advantage.

INDUSTRY ENVIRONMENT

If a company's past record of growth and profitability meets your criteria, you should subject it to a second standard: Does it operate in an industry environment conducive to supporting a high rate of growth? Computer Associates, for instance, certainly owes a lot of its growth to its favorable environment and meets this standard easily. The late T. Rowe Price, one of the great practicioners of growth stock investing, always referred to this characteristic as the fertility of the field. He believed that it's usually much easier for a company to grow along with its competitors in a favorable industry environment than it is to slug it out for market share in a slow growth business.

As you think about the fertility of an industry, it's useful to remember that many small companies grow fast because they can exploit some kind of change—demographic, economic, political, social, or technological. For instance, McDonald's couldn't have become one of the great emerging growth companies of its day unless our society had first developed a suburbanized, automobile-dependent life-style that would support fast-food drive-in restaurants.

Another socioeconomic change with important business implications has been the growing number of women in the workplace. This has made rapid growth possible for specialty retailers, like The Limited, who have targeted this specific niche market within the broad spectrum of the retailing industry.

In terms of pure economics, the big increase in oil prices that OPEC engineered in the late 1970s is an example of a change that is still having repercussions. Higher crude prices shifted profitability away from the refining and marketing end of the oil business and caused the major companies to shut down many of their service stations. This left a void that made it a lot easier for companies like Jiffy Lube, which specializes in quick oil changes, to grow rapidly.

Even in relatively mature and stable sectors of the economy, like the food industry, technological change has spawned opportunity for emerging growth companies. Golden Valley Microwave Foods, for instance, couldn't have achieved its spectacular growth unless a proliferation of microwave ovens had taken place first. In a way, Golden Valley has a lot in common with software companies like Lotus, Ashton-Tate, and MicroSoft. All of them are exploiting the market opportunity created by the development of new hardware. In Golden Valley's case, it just happens to be microwave ovens instead of personal computers.

From McDonald's to Golden Valley, these growth companies have all been the beneficiaries of some kind of change. But clearly, the one area of our society where change is taking place rapidly is technology. As a result, many small technology companies meet the industry environment standard easily, and it's not unusual to see these stocks representing 50% or more of the assets in some emerging growth portfolios. However, weightings this high create unnecessary risk. In the next chapter we'll discuss two technology companies that operated in apparently fertile industry environments but had other characteristics that made them prone to some very common problems. Both experienced earnings shortfalls that led to disappointing stock performance.

FRAGMENTED INDUSTRIES

An industry environment that is favorable to good growth isn't always obvious. Some companies are able to achieve high growth in businesses that appear to be mature and slow growing. They operate in fragmented industries, where they can establish an edge over the hundreds of relatively weak, unsophisticated companies they compete against. Rapid growth in this kind of environment is usually achieved through a strategy of industry consolidation: supplementing internal growth with acquisitions and eventually reaching a size that allows a measure of dominance.

InSpeech is a good example of a company following this strategy. It provides speech therapy and physical therapy services. InSpeech's teams of trained practicioners call on nursing homes, where they help stroke victims and other handicapped patients to recover some of their speaking ability and lead more normal lives.

This industry is full of small mom and pop operators who conduct their practice in a limited, local market. They typically have annual revenue of well under $1 million and think of themselves as therapists first and businessmen second, if at all. It's exactly the kind of environment that John Foster, InSpeech's chairman, loves to operate in. He has had an enviable record of success with other companies in similarly fragmented businesses, the most notable being Foster Medical, which was acquired by Avon.

Foster's goal is to "McDonaldize" the speech therapy business by implementing a carefully developed system for running all of the company's local practices. This basic pattern, which includes detailed operating procedures and financial control systems, has been thoroughly tested and refined through acquisitions that InSpeech has already made. It's designed to be duplicated in cookie-cutter fashion, serving as a framework for integrating future acquisitions, with which the company will continue to augment its internal growth. InSpeech is well positioned to pursue this strategy because its public ownership gives it good access to financing. It's a strategy that's applicable only to fragmented industries, but it will sometimes allow an apparently mundane business to grow at rates that even the most exotic technology company would envy.

COMPETITION

To characterize an industry environment as fragmented is really just a way of commenting on its competitive environment, which in itself is another important stock selection standard. Common sense as well as basic economic theory dictates that highly competitive businesses with low barriers to entry usually have anemic profit margins and eventually undergo industry shakeouts. This happened with computer disk drives, an industry whose growth prospects seemed so bright in the early 1980s that it attracted gobs of venture capital money for funding startups. Unfortunately, the field wasn't quite fertile enough to accomodate the hundred or so companies that set out to dominate it.

The tricky part about evaluating companies in terms of their competitive environment is fine tuning your standards. If your criteria are too stringent, you could end up with a portfolio of just six stocks, all of which are cable TV companies. (The economics of this business are such that cable companies, much like utilities, typically operate without direct competition in their own local market.) On the other hand, if your criteria are too loose, you'll own a lot of companies that are second-rate competitors in commodity-like businesses. So this standard requires judgment and doesn't lend itself to a formula approach.

Nevertheless, there are a few questions you should always consider. One is the nature of the competition. It's often better to be in an industry with hundreds of weak competitors than one with a handful of strong competitors. For instance, InSpeech has more competitors than any semiconductor manufacturer, but no one would seriously argue that it is in a more competitive business.

Another question concerns the company's position relative to actual or potential competitors. An industry leader with a proprietary product or a significant cost advantage should have operating margins of 20% or more. By comparison, a me-too company with a low market share and no meaningful competitive edge may have margins as low as 5%. Now if another competitor decides to enter the market and cut prices, the weaker company may find its profitability wiped out practically overnight. Of course, the industry leader will also be hurt, but his higher margins will cushion the impact. For instance, if prices are suddenly cut by 5%, the leader's margin will still be around 15%, but the me-too company may be lucky to break even.

In a new industry it's often difficult to decide which of two or more companies is really better positioned to eventually become the leader. For a long time, investors and analysts argued the relative merits of Daisy Systems versus Mentor Graphics in computer-aided engineering, and Sun Microsystems versus Apollo in workstations. In this kind of situation, institutional investors often take a "package approach." They buy both stocks, hoping to identify the strong company and eliminate the weak one before the difference becomes apparent to the market. The problem with this strategy is that sometimes the difference becomes glaringly obvious to everyone at the same time: One of the companies reports a bad quarter, and its stock gets clobbered.

Yet there are industries where a package approach does make sense. For instance, biotechnology is still such an embryonic business that there is really no way to know which companies will be successful in the research lab and which will be first to obtain regulatory approval to market their products. So spreading the bet over a number of stocks is a reasonable tactic. However, in most cases, there's little reason to take a package approach. It's usually better to focus on a smaller number of companies that really are one of a kind. Again, don't forfeit your ability to be selective.

MANAGEMENT

The quality of management obviously has a strong influence on the success or failure of any business. Some investors consider it far and away more important than any other factor. But evaluating management is always very subjective and difficult. Even securities analysts, who invariably have much better access than individual investors, are often so wide of the mark that their assessments seem to be almost random. The problem stems from the fact that many small companies grow rapidly, at least for a while, simply because they operate in an extraordinarily fertile business environment. A hot new product that is growing spectacularly and doesn't yet have much competition can cover up a host of management shortcomings. When a company is fortunate enough to be in this position, it's often hard to tell if its growth is because of, or in spite of, its management. Is the newly recruited sales force really an exceptionally talented and motivated group, or are they just overpaid order takers? Has the company developed technology that is truly state-of-the-art, or does it just have a temporary edge that will be hard to defend and soon be lost? Are profit margins likely to remain high because the product is really proprietary, or are they at a level that will prove unsustainable as the market becomes more competitive? Learning the answers to these questions is often very expensive.

One way to get a handle on how good a company and its management really are is to talk to the people who know it best—customers, suppliers, and competitors. Contacting them and then getting them to speak openly and frankly isn't easy, but the insights they can provide are sometimes invaluable. As an analyst, I've found this practice to be well worth the effort on a number of occasions. And after reading John Love's *McDonald's Behind the Arches*, I am convinced an investor who had gone through this process with franchisees, competitors, and suppliers, at the time of Mc-Donald's initial public offering would have developed strong confidence in the sustainability of that company's growth. Imagine what an edge this would have given you relative to the average investor, who no doubt thought of it as just another hamburger stand.

But it's unusual to get this kind of insight. Overall, I believe that good companies make good managements, rather than the other way around. So I prefer to invest in businesses that are inherently attractive; they can grow without having extraordinarily gifted managements. Not only are they more likely to succeed, but they're easier to identify.

BEYOND THE BASICS

The four basic stock selection standards we have discussed—past growth and profitability, industry environment, competition, and management—are important tools. Every serious emerging growth investor should use them, even if only on an informal basis. If they are applied diligently and with good judgment, it's reasonable to expect at least half the stocks in a portfolio to come close to or meet earnings expectations. This may not be a spectacularly high success ratio, but it's a lot better than the percentage of repeaters on the *Business Week* list. And it should allow a high enough return relative to the overall market to compensate for the extra risk you're assuming. But it still leaves plenty of room for improvement. As we'll discuss in the next chapter, it's necessary to go beyond these basic standards to realize the full potential of emerging growth investing.

4

Tough Businesses and
Common Problems

Although the stock selection standards discussed in the last chapter are important investment tools, they're only a starting point; they are far from being the whole answer to the problem. Many small companies meet these basic standards easily—they have good records and strong financials, operate in a fertile industry environment, have limited competition, and are run by reasonably competent managements—and yet they still stumble badly and turn out to be poor investments. In this chapter we'll discuss three common problems that cause many apparently attractive emerging growth companies to fall short of investors' expectations. We'll also discuss the characteristics that make some companies particularly vulnerable to these problems. Learning to recognize these kinds of companies is important because it will help you to avoid beating yourself.

Have you ever watched one of those classic tennis matches in which a wily old veteran defeats an opponent who is 20 or even 30 years younger? The veteran overcomes the younger player's physical advantages by chipping away at his weaknesses, until eventually he makes so many mistakes that he ends up beating himself. The veteran doesn't serve as many aces as the younger player, but he never double faults. He hits very few shots that are outright winners, but it's even more rare for him to commit an unforced error. The key to the veteran's success is that he doesn't beat himself. To avoid beating yourself at emerging growth investing, you have to steer clear of tough businesses and the common problems that trip up so many small companies.

Sometimes companies produce disappointing earnings and poor stock performance because they are blindsided by events that are completely external to them. For instance, a gaggle of new competitors may suddenly enter the market. Or a dramatic new development in technology makes their product obsolete overnight. These are the kinds of problems that many people believe are the common risks of emerging growth investing. But actually they're quite rare. I've seen a lot of small companies deliver earnings shortfalls; most often they're the result of internal management errors. For every company blindsided by outside events, there are probably 10 that disappoint investors because they shoot themselves in the foot.

Usually these companies are not run by spectacularly inept managements. But they are in businesses that are tough to run—businesses where even a competent management team is prone to making serious errors. As an institutional portfolio manager, I had particularly memorable investments in two such companies: Zycad and Hogan Systems. What makes them memorable isn't the money I lost with them, but the fact that they so easily met the four stock selection criteria we discussed in the last chapter. In spite of meeting these standards, they turned out to be poor investments. Looking back, I realize the problems these companies encountered were classics that plague many emerging growth companies.

Zycad's basic weakness was lack of visibility, which made its business tough to plan and control. And its difficulties were compounded by a lengthening sales cycle. Hogan Systems stumbled badly because it was too dependent on a new product, which it introduced prematurely. And both companies made their problems worse by attempting to grow at rates that were just unrealistically high.

LACK OF VISIBILITY

Zycad is a small, high-tech company that experienced a serious earnings shortfall because it vastly overestimated the size of its market. This is not an unusual mistake among small companies that sell a high-priced product that incorporates substantial new technology. It may have something to do with the fact that these companies are often run by engineers, who sometimes become so enraptured with their product's technology that they get carried away into making unrealistically optimistic projections of its sales potential.

Zycad's product line consists of a family of high-performance super-computers that facilitate the design of complex electronic circuits. By performing logic and fault simulation, they eliminate many time-consuming bottlenecks in the design cycle and allow the user to begin manufacturing a new product much sooner than would otherwise be possible. Being quick to market is usually an important advantage in the electronics business. But most of Zycad's products sell for more than $500,000 a copy, so the decision to purchase one is not taken lightly, no matter how great the perceived benefits may be.

Zycad was founded in 1981 and remained in the development stage until 1983. In that year, the company booked revenue of $4.1 million and managed to record pretax margins of better than 20%, even though it didn't begin to make shipments until the second half of the year. With its product finally perfected, Zycad was off to a flying start.

In spite of the sluggish demand environment that most technology companies were beginning to struggle with at the time, Zycad's momentum remained strong, allowing it to successfully complete an initial public offering in June 1984. Even though investor interest in emerging growth technology stocks had been falling precipitously over the preceding 12 months, Zycad was able to raise nearly $30 million by selling stock at a price of $15, almost 30x that year's earnings.

Zycad's sales and earnings record is shown in Table 4.1. In 1984, its first year as a public company, growth was nothing less than sensational. Earnings increased more than fivefold from $.09 to $.51 per share. But just a year later profitability fell apart. Earnings dropped from $.51 to $.19 in 1985, and only a scant $.03 of the total represented operating income. The other $.16 came from interest income earned on the money raised by the initial public offering plus a small tax credit. The company's operating margin fell from an unusually high level of 33.1%, almost all the way down to breakeven. This collapse in operating profitability was particularly stunning because it occurred in a year when sales grew by nearly 38%. It's safe to say that 99 out of 100 companies would have been delighted with this kind of sales growth.

Zycad's earnings collapse wasn't the result of some new competitor coming into the market and slashing prices. In fact, the company actually increased prices halfway through the year. Instead, profits crumbled because costs increased at a much faster rate than sales. Management increased the research and development staff and raised overhead much too quickly. These disastrous decisions were made because the company based its budget on a sales forecast that turned out to be unrealistically optimistic.

TABLE 4.1 Zycad

Year	1983	1984	1985
Sales	$4,101	$19,443	$26,776
Cost of Goods Sold	1,086	3,094	5,898
Gross Profit	3,015	16,349	20,878
Operating Expenses			
Sales and Marketing	556	4,320	9,289
Research and Development	1,284	3,323	7,220
General and Administrative	555	2,265	4,035
Operating Income	621	6,442	333
Net Interest Income	218	1,880	1,687
Pretax Income	839	8,325	2,020
Tax	398	3,120	(150)
Net Income	$ 441	$ 5,205	$ 2,170
Earnings per Share	$.05	$.51	$.19
Percentage of Total Revenue			
Sales	100.0%	100.0%	100.0%
Cost of Goods Sold	26.5	15.9	22.0
Gross Profit	73.5	84.1	78.0
Sales and Marketing	13.6	22.2	34.7
Research and Development	31.3	17.1	27.0
General and Administrative	13.5	11.7	15.1
Total Operating Expense	58.4	51.0	76.8
Operating Income	15.1%	33.1%	1.2%

Although sales rose by nearly 38%, both marketing expense and research spending more than doubled. This pushed the operating expense ratio up to 76.8% of sales, compared to 51.0% the year before. With expenses at such a high level, there simply wasn't any room left for the company to earn meaningful profits.

To have maintained its operating margin at the same level as the prior year, Zycad would have needed revenue of around $50 million, versus the $27 million it actually booked. Management's expectations were obviously way off the mark. At the time the company was setting budgets, management believed the potential market was around $800 million. If this estimate had been accurate, a sales forecast well in excess of $27 million would have been reasonable, but the market proved to be nowhere near this big.

Undoubtedly, the product's strong initial acceptance had a lot to do with the overly optimistic sales forecast. In fact, Zycad's early shipments were made to a handful of highly receptive, leading-edge customers who were unusually anxious to try out the new technology. To some extent, management realized this. They referred to these pioneer-spirited early customers as "low fruit" because they were so enthusiastic about the product's capabilities that it was practically a cinch to sell them one or two units. What management badly misjugded was just how high and how sparse the rest of the fruit on the tree would turn out to be.

This happens quite frequently to high-tech companies introducing a totally new product for which there is no pre-existing market. A small part of the market is comprised of pioneers—early users who believe the new technology will help them and are highly receptive to it. The rest of the market is made up of cautious skeptics, who see a lot of potential risk in adopting almost any new technology. The gap between the two groups often turns out to be wider than expected; and unfortunately, the skeptics always outnumber the pioneers by a wide margin. These prospects must be totally convinced that the technology is not only cost-effective but also that it can be implemented smoothly and that it can be applied to their own specific needs. Additionally, they must feel comfortable that the manufacturer will remain in business and be able to service and support the product. In effect, the person making the purchase decision may be betting his job that an obscure, young company will be able to deliver on its promises. Nobody ever gets fired for buying from IBM, but with Zycad, who knows?

On top of this career risk, capital budget constraints may keep prospective customers from buying the new equipment, even after they have become fully convinced of its virtues. At worst these prospects never materialize into customers. At best they create a lengthening sales cycle.

LENGTHENING SALES CYCLES

The sales cycle is the length of time it takes to turn a prospect into a customer. For most service companies and most consumer product companies, the sales cycle is so short that it is not an issue. The buyer of a McDonald's hamburger, for instance, isn't likely to deliberate long over his purchase decision or defer making it. However, expensive high-tech products are anything but an impulse purchase. In addition to commiting a significant amount of money, the company buying them may have to hire and train people to use the new equipment and must often make changes in existing systems and procedures to accomodate it. So the cost of implementing new technology is often much greater than just the price tag of the hardware. Therefore, it's unusual for these decisions to be made without a lot of study and without review at more than one level of the organization. As a result, it may take 6 months or more from the time a high-tech company identifies a prospect to the time it closes the sale.

A company whose sales cycle suddenly increases from, say, 6 months to 9 months will be hard pressed to avoid a shortfall in sales and earnings. This is a particularly insidious problem because at the same time that sales and earnings are falling short of budget, the prospect list is actually getting longer. Therefore, it's very easy for management to rationalize delaying the painful expense reductions that are necessary to preserve profit margins. There is always the hope that next month or next quarter enough deals will be closed to make up the current shortfall. So usually nothing is done until it is too late to save earnings, and more often than not the shareholders end up getting bagged.

Zycad's earnings collapse started because its business lacked visibility and management prepared its plans and budgets based on a forecast that was grossly inaccurate. Then a lengthening sales cycle froze it into inaction. By the time management recognized that its revenue expectations had been unrealistic and that overhead had been set at much too high a level, it was too late. The business was already out of control, and earnings were in an irreversible dive.

In trying to avoid companies likely to run into the same problems Zycad experienced, a good warning sign to stay alert for is a high-priced product. Companies that sell big ticket items are the most susceptible to lengthening sales cycles. Their businesses are also the hardest to forecast,

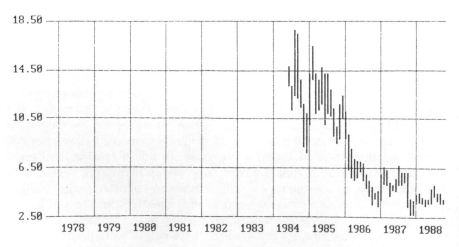

Figure 4.1. Zycad Corporation stock chart. Courtesy of Bridge Information Systems, Inc.

particularly if their product incorporates substantial new technology that many of the prospective customers may not be anxious to accept.

NEW PRODUCT DEPENDENCE

When it becomes apparent that an earnings shortfall is developing, some managements will do almost anything to prevent it and keep near-term earnings on target. More than one small company has actually become so obsessed with "making the numbers" that it has borrowed from future quarters, booking sales in *anticipation* of orders. But cooking the books like this to deliver earnings is quite rare. It's much more common that emerging growth companies try to preserve short-term earnings with moves that impair their long-term growth. This is what happened to Hogan Systems in 1984 and 1985. The company's continued growth was almost totally dependent on a new product, which it introduced prematurely in an effort to preserve its record and maintain its credibility with analysts.

Hogan is in the business of developing and marketing applications software systems for large banks and thrift institutions. Like Zycad, Hogan estimated its potential market to be very large, and it had little direct competition. Another similarity was the high price of its products. Some of Hogan's larger contracts carried price tags of nearly $2 million. The timing of delivery inevitably caused a great deal of lumpiness in its quarterly results. Revenues would fluctuate wildly, while costs remained constant, whether 1 system or 20 systems were shipped. Slippage of a contract or two from one quarter into the next always had a big impact on earnings.

Through the first 9 months of its March 1984 fiscal year, Hogan's earnings were actually trailing the previous year at $.19 per share versus $.26. In spite of the unfavorable comparison for this period, however, the stock performed reasonably well because management encouraged analysts to expect a really strong fourth quarter. To deliver on this implicit promise, Hogan was counting on a big contribution from the initial shipments of its Loans System, a new software product. Even by Hogan's high standards, Loans was a very large and complex system. It took a team of the company's best programmers over 3 years to write it, and it contained over half a million lines of code. Hogan embarked on this project with a lot of input and support from banks who were already users of its other software products. So, well before the software was complete, the company already had commitments to ship about 30 systems as soon as they became available.

Hogan was just able to get these shipments out the door before the close of the quarter, and it delivered earnings that pleased even the most bullish analysts. The fourth quarter numbers came in at $.36 per share, up from $.10 in the comparable period. This gave the company a growth rate of better than 50% for the full year.

Unfortunately, however, the Loans System contained some very serious bugs that Hogan had not taken time to remedy because of the pressure to keep its promises to the analysts and meet its short-term earnings goals. Even more important, installation of the system turned out to require much greater support than Hogan was capable of providing. These problems soon became widely known throughout the banking community, and Hogan was suddenly unable to get the favorable referrals that had always been an important part of its sales effort. As a result of the Loans debacle, sales of software products actually fell by 43% in fiscal 1985, and Hogan incurred a pretax loss of more than $20 million.

Near the end of the 1985 fiscal year, the company hosted a small meeting for analysts and large institutional shareholders. Here is how management assessed the problems it was facing:

> As you know, we reported a fairly substantial operating loss [for the third quarter] which we attributed primarily to a lack of software sales, as a result of sales cycle lengthening. We have a substantial prospect list, but it's taken longer to close them than we've experienced in the past. There seems to be a comfort or credibility issue among prospects. There's been some concern, especially among the newer buyers, about the level of service they can expect to receive from us. And there's a developing perception that in order for a bank or thrift to be successful implementing our software they need more direct involvement from Hogan.
>
> Another concern is that we've damaged our credibility by delivering the Loans System to a very large number of clients and we weren't prepared, and didn't realize we needed to be prepared, to be heavily involved with all of those clients. So we got too many of them out there too quickly. Plus, there are some additional features in the mortgage arena that we either didn't design into the system because we didn't think they were immediately necessary or where a new loan instrument was invented after we froze the design of the Loans System. So there are some features, especially commercial banks need to have in the system to be able to implement it.
>
> So the combination of those things has kind of slowed the whole process down. Most of what we counted on closing in the third quarter has not gone away, but now there are fourth-quarter issues. Banks don't want to buy software from a company they would not loan money to. And the fact that we lost money in the third quarter is causing them to ask a new set of questions before they come to the sales close.

In hindsight, it's easy to see that Hogan made a serious mistake in succumbing to the self-induced pressure to meet short-term earnings targets. If the Loans System hadn't been shipped prematurely, at least not in such large numbers, the program bugs might have been easier to correct. Certainly, the installation and support problems would have been much less severe. And Hogan's reputation within the banking community would not have been so badly tarnished. Earnings would most likely have been down, but the debacle that actually took place could have been avoided.

Small companies that allow themselves to become so dependent on the successful introduction of a new product are always risky. In Hogan's case, it was easy to overlook this basic fact. After all, it had 30 banks lined up and waiting to buy the Loans System. Most analysts expected it to be a slam dunk. But new products never are.

GROWING TOO FAST

Both Hogan and Zycad compounded their basic problems by committing another error that is common to emerging growth companies. They set growth rate targets—well in excess of 30%—that were simply beyond their grasp. Even though their markets might have been fertile enough to support this kind of growth, they were still unrealistic targets in terms of the organizational strains they created and in terms of the management resources the companies had available.

It is very important to understand that the faster a company attempts to grow, the more likely it is to get out of control, stumble, and disappoint

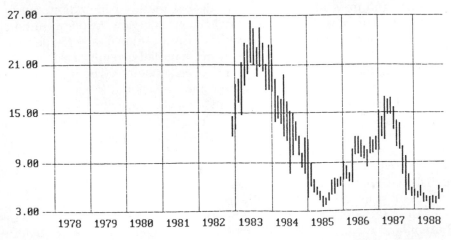

Figure 4.2. Hogan Systems Inc. stock chart. Courtesy of Bridge Information Systems, Inc.

investors. Consider that a company growing at a 30% rate must double its employee count about every 2½ years. Just in terms of recruitment and training, this represents a formidable challenge. If, for example, a company starts with 10 salesmen, it must hire and train 3 more next year, 4 the following year, and 5 more the year after that for a total of 12. Even more will be needed if any of the original 10 leave the company or are promoted. And how likely is it that the last 3 salesmen hired will be as good as the first 3?

Now consider the same company's requirements if it is growing at 15% rather than 30%. Instead of needing 12 new salesmen over a 3-year period, it would need only 5. At this lower growth rate, the challenge of recruiting, training, and assimilating the new salesmen into the organization would obviously be a great deal less demanding.

The need to expand capacity is another aspect of exceptionally high growth that intensifies strain and increases fundamental risk. In a manufacturing business, new plants or at least new machinery and assembly lines must be brought onstream. In a service business, it's usually necessary to enter additional geographic markets by opening new regional offices. These expansions always carry startup risk, and the new operations may incur losses for much longer than expected.

Also, many small companies find it necessary to develop new channels of distribution to support high growth. Often a network of manufacturers' representatives has to be supplemented or even replaced by a direct sales force. This kind of change is likely to cause at least a temporary loss of business as the reps give the product line less attention, maybe even dropping it altogether. In time the direct sales force will probably pick up the slack and may ultimately achieve deeper market penetration, but for the first few months, its productivity is likely to be low. In the meantime, overhead will be rising rapidly because of the additional salary expense of the new salesmen. If the transition is not handled carefully, sales growth will start to flatten out just as cost increases accelerate. The inevitable result will be a squeeze on profit margins and disappointing earnings.

New distribution channels, expanded plant capacity, more working capital, and all the other prerequisites for growth require investment. So the faster a company grows, the more likely it is to need external capital to finance these essential investments. And as a company turns to the equity market more frequently, shareholder dilution and the cost of capital usually go up. So financing represents yet another hurdle that small companies must negotiate successfully to sustain a high growth rate.

All of these obstacles to growth—personnel, physical capacity, distribution, and financing—represent serious management challenges that increase in complexity as a company grows. For instance, at the $20 million sales level, lots of companies can get by with a good accountant as their only financial officer, but when sales rise to $50 million, a whole new set of problems usually arise. A standard cost system may be needed to keep manufacturing costs in line. Accounts receivable and inventory control are likely to become much more complex. Banking relationships will probably require much greater sophistication. Knowledge of foreign currency markets may even become necessary if the company attempts to expand into overseas markets. All of these new requirements will almost certainly demand that the company recruit a stronger chief financial officer with experience in these areas. And this is just one example of the kinds of management changes an emerging growth company has to make to sustain and control its growth. Similar changes will also have to be made in sales, marketing, manufacturing, and research—virtually every critical area of the business—if the company is to avoid outgrowing its management.

Unfortunately, there is no convenient rule of thumb for determining how fast is too fast. For one thing, size has a lot to do with it. At the $10 million sales level, a company may be able to handle a 50% growth rate with relatively little strain. By the time it has reached $100 million, the same company may have a hard time handling 25% growth. Visibility also has a lot to do with setting the limits on growth. The more predictable a company's business, the better able it is to maintain control in spite of the strains of high growth.

BLAMING IT ON MANAGEMENT

When a company stumbles badly and experiences a severe earnings shortfall as Zycad and Hogan did, investors often turn nasty and look for a target on which they can vent their frustrations. Management is invariably the most obvious and the most convenient scapegoat. Analysts tell their institutional clients they're not sure if the company has intentionally misled them, or if it's just not as well managed as they had thought. Most investors aren't likely to sit around debating which answer is correct. They figure it makes little difference whether the CEO is dishonest or merely stupid. Either way they're better off not owning the stock.

This is certainly the way a lot of investors (and probably directors too) reacted when Zycad and Hogan disappointed them. Not surprisingly, the CEOs of both companies resigned soon after the full extent of their problems became evident. Were they really bumbling incompetents who found themselves out of their depth and destroyed shareholder wealth through blunders that more able managers would have easily avoided? I don't think so. Unquestionably, they made some serious errors of judgment, but it seems more likely they were somewhere around average in their ability, rather than the bunglers some angry investors made them out to be. However, they were running tough businesses that were particularly prone to the very mistakes they made. The true size of their markets was difficult to judge. The high price of their products caused lengthening sales cycles, and lack of visibility made their businesses very hard to control. On top of this, both companies compounded their problems by setting internal growth targets that were beyond their grasp. It was easy for investors to blame management for these problems, but this was really a cop-out. The businesses were just too tough to permit the kind of growth that management and investors thought was possible.

The glamour of new technology and the allure of spectacular growth is a combination that's hard to resist. But it can often disguise a business that's a lot tougher than either management or investors ever anticipated. And if growth targets are set unrealistically high, as is so often the case, it's very easy to lose control. Be careful of these companies for they often turn out to be disappointing investments.

5

Visibility and Recurring Revenue

The best way to avoid disappointing investments like Zycad and Hogan is to concentrate on companies that operate in a more benign business environment. They don't need to be run by a management genius or have extraordinarily good luck to achieve consistently high earnings growth. And your odds of making money with this type of investment are much better.

These companies remind me of a passage from *Mortal Splendor: The American Empire in Transition* (Houghton Mifflin, 1987, p. 54), a book in which Walter Russell Mead characterizes contemporary America as an empire in decline. In his analysis, Mead makes the following observation:

> The tides of history created the American Empire. For most of its history the United States has not had outstanding leadership in its government, yet this lack did not prevent America's rise to power.

Just as a nation may be able to rise to a position of prominence without having outstanding leadership, some small companies are able to achieve excellent records of sustained growth without having exceptional managements. This is because they're in businesses that are relatively easy to manage.

There are a lot of different elements that go into managing a company, and a lot of different styles that have led to success. For instance, Ross

Perot's ability to motivate his managers and employees was the hallmark of his charismatic leadership at EDS. Ray Kroc's obsession with operational detail was probably his most important contribution to McDonald's growth. Harold Geneen's insistence on careful planning and tight controls allowed IT&T to keep growing long after most conglomerates had proved themselves too awkward and unwieldy. And Seymour Cray's genius for product development was the main contributor to Cray Research's ascent to dominance in the field of supercomputers. All of these companies enjoyed notable success under CEOs with very different styles and strengths.

However, the one attribute that does more than any other to assure management success is the ability to anticipate future conditions accurately. A CEO who has a clear picture of his company's future enjoys an enormous edge; he can act in advance to make sure it's well prepared ahead of time. He can see that the necessary production facilities, technology, distribution channels, marketing strategies, and management organization are all in place as they are needed. A manager with the ability to anticipate accurately doesn't have to be exceptional in any other categories to lead his company successfully.

There is tremendous variation across industries and companies as to how easy or difficult it is to anticipate the future. Companies that lend themselves well to accurate anticipation have what investors often refer to as good visibility. Running one of them is a lot like driving along a superhighway in light traffic on a clear day. You have to pay attention and be careful, but it's not difficult to move fast. Good visibility and room to maneuver allow you to easily avoid any hazard that might be on the road. Whether you are driving along a highway or trying to run an emerging growth company, visibility and room to maneuver make the job a lot easier.

HIGH-VISIBILITY BUSINESSES

Some companies enjoy good visibility because they provide a service that their customers can be counted on to use again and again. A good example is Caremark, a small company that achieved excellent growth for a number of years and then was bought out by Baxter-Travenol in 1987. Caremark helped to pioneer development of home infusion therapy, a service that makes it possible for seriously ill people to receive nutrient liquids, antibiotics, or I-V drug solutions at home. Without home infusion therapy, these people would have to remain in the hospital to receive the same treatment. So pressure to hold the line on health care costs by reducing the length of hospital stays has benefited Caremark significantly. And most patients would rather be treated at home anyway.

Unfortunately, every day thousands of people contract cancer, AIDS, diabetes, and other serious diseases, thus becoming eventual candidates for home infusion therapy. Treatment is not something they can put off, the way you can defer buying a new car or a second VCR. So companies like Caremark that are involved in the treatment of these diseases generally have a very good handle on what their market is going to look like tomorrow, as well as today. Current patients have to continue receiving treatment, and the laws of probability assure a steady stream of new patients in the future.

Companies that manufacture a consumable product often possess a similar element of repeat business. A good example is Neutrogena, a manufacturer of very high-quality skin-care soap that enjoys strong brand loyalty. Although the soap business is competitive and commodity-like for the most part, Neutrogena has attained dominance in its own market niche. And the loyalty of its customers, combined with the consumable nature of its product, endows it with good visibility.

Other types of emerging growth companies have good visibility because of their backlogs. For instance, the Pentagon relies heavily on outside contractors to supply most of its software and computer services. Many of the small companies involved in this business are well entrenched and have strong contract protection because the sophisticated services they provide are critically important. They derive good visibility from their long backlogs and the knowledge that their major customer is highly dependent on them, even when there is pressure on the budget.

RECURRING REVENUE

The strongest kind of visibility is derived from a recurring revenue base— a business segment that will go on generating a stream of revenue for as long as it is managed reasonably well. Remember how Computer Associates, discussed in the first chapter, offered short-term licenses on many of its software products. Although there was no contractual obligation, the company knew it could rely on its customers to renew the licenses almost automatically. So this strategy created a recurring revenue base, which has been very helpful in allowing Computer Associates to maintain its pattern of consistent growth.

A classic example of a recurring revenue business is cable television. The customers are literally hooked into a cable system, paying a monthly fee for the service. A few years ago a friend of my son moved to a part of town that wasn't served by cable. The boy complained long and bitterly about this deprivation. Most cable subscribers feel the same way; they are no more likely to drop the service than they are to stop buying electricity, water, telephone service, or any other utility. In fact, about the only way a cable company loses a subscriber is if he dies or, like my son's friend, moves away. This certainty provides the cable operator the visibility he needs to project revenue well into the future with a high degree of confidence—something that is extremely helpful in planning, controlling, and financing the business as well as managing day-to-day operations.

Another type of business that generates significant amounts of recurring revenue is the manufacturing of disposables that have a razor blade aspect to them. Checkpoint Systems illustrates this kind of recurring revenue company. It manufactures electronic surveillance systems, most of which it sells to retail merchants, who use them to prevent shoplifting. The systems consist of radio wave transmitters and disposable tags that are attached to the store's merchandise. Unless the tag is deactivated before an item is taken out of the store, it interferes with the radio transmission, and this sets off an alarm. Unlike some of its competitors, who use large plastic devices, Checkpoint has based its system on disposable paper tags. These look very much like a price tag and are sometimes actually used for that purpose. Because the tags must be deactivated and cannot be reused, every item the retailer sells automatically creates demand for another tag. So Checkpoint continues to sell tags to the retailer for as long as the system remains in use. These ongoing tag sales generate a stream of recurring revenue that is about equal to the revenue from sales of new systems. New system sales tend to have irregular timing, bouncing up and down from one quarter to the next with very little predictability. The tag sales add an important element of stability, helping to smooth out the business.

Another of these razor blade companies is Scan-Tron, a manufacturer of optical mark reading equipment and forms, which it sells primarily to the education market. Teachers from grade school to college use these systems for automatically grading multiple choice tests. In addition to saving time, they provide quick feedback on how well students have absorbed various parts of their lessons, pointing the way to material that needs more coverage. As a result of the system's popularity with teachers, Scan-Tron can project the volume of form sales each installation will generate with a high degree of confidence. Not only does this provide a base of recurring revenue, it has also enabled the company to adopt a strategy of loaning the machines at no charge in return for a minimum commitment on form sales. In effect, Scan-Tron gives away the razor so it can sell more blades.

Franchising is still another type of business that produces a recurring revenue base for some emerging growth companies. This way of doing business has some very attractive characteristics when it is properly executed. To start, the people a company can attract to become franchisees are usually much more competent and ambitious than the people it can hire as employees. Because the franchisee actually owns his own business, he has plenty of motivation to make it succeed—much more than an employee would. In addition, the franchisees supply most of the capital that is needed to finance growth. By sharing the problems of management and financing with franchisees, a company can grow faster than would be possible if it owned all of its units.

To make the partnership work, however, the franchisor must also supply some essential ingredients. To start, the basic concept must be valid, or the franchisees won't be able to build a solid business. Beyond that, the franchisor must provide training and well-tested systems and procedures for actually making the concept work. And once the franchisee's business is up and running, it will need some ongoing support in marketing and operations. Unless the franchisees feel they are getting a fair deal, it will be difficult for the company to keep on growing because new franchises will be hard to sell.

Franchising lends itself particularly well to businesses like restaurants and retailing, which can support a large number of outlets that are similar but geographically dispersed. It's a natural strategy for an emerging growth company like Jiffy Lube, whose goal is to become the McDonald's of the quick oil-change business. In addition to making rapid expansion possible, franchising also provides Jiffy Lube with several major streams of recurring revenue. The most important of these is the ongoing royalty fee, which the franchisees pay monthly. This fee, which is set at a fixed percentage of the franchisee's revenue, will grow as the number of units increases and as sales by existing franchisees grow.

Another stream of recurring revenue comes from sales of motor oil, filters, and other supplies that the franchisees buy from Jiffy Lube. Also, Jiffy Lube owns many of the physical units themselves and rents them to the franchisees. Like royalties and sales of supplies, this rental income is another recurring revenue source that will continue for as long as the franchisees remain in business. Actually, Jiffy Lube's only revenue source that is not recurring is the initial fee a franchisee pays when he opens up his business. These fees will obviously dry up when the company stops selling new franchises, but so too will a lot of the associated selling and pre-opening expenses.

EASING THE BURDEN ON MANAGEMENT

The good visibility that comes from a large base of recurring revenue makes the job of keeping a rapidly growing company under control much easier. Recurring revenue provides the following advantages:

1. More accurate forecasting and tighter control.
2. Easier and more controllable growth.
3. Less dependence on new products.
4. The ability to mature gracefully from a financial perspective.

A recurring revenue company should always have a very good idea of how much capacity it needs to add and how many new employees it should hire to accommodate its growth. So its overhead expenses are unlikely to get out of control and go unabsorbed. Remember how Zycad's operating expenses increased more than 100%, while sales were only growing at a 38% rate. Because of an inaccurate sales forecast, management allowed overhead to expand too fast, and margins were crushed. This should never happen to a company that has good visibility. With a significant base of recurring revenue, Zycad could have forecast its sales with reasonable accuracy. Expense levels would probably never have gotten so far out of line.

In addition to being easier to plan, recurring revenue businesses very often have a cookie-cutter simplicity. This makes their day-to-day operations more manageable and their growth easier and more controllable. In the case of Jiffy Lube, for instance, one franchise unit is essentially the same as all the others. Recruiting, training, and launching new franchisees—the key to continued growth—is something the company has already done successfully hundreds of times. So continuing to grow doesn't demand much change or create enormous strain. For example, if the company sold and opened, say, 50 new units last year, it already has in place the staff and organization necessary to do the same number again this year. And with more experience than they had a year ago, the staff may even be able to do a better job of recruiting qualified franchise candidates, helping them to find good locations, and providing effective training and support.

If the company just continues to sell and open the same number of new units each year, its rate of growth will taper off as the base becomes larger. But there will still be positive growth because each year starts from a base that's about equal to the prior year's sales. And even in a year when it doesn't sell a single new unit, the company may still be able to grow slightly if the average sales per franchise increase.

This kind of growth is simple and easy to control, especially in comparison to companies that lack a significant base of recurring revenue. A typical high-tech emerging growth company without a recurring revenue base—for instance a manufacturer of semiconductor chips, or medical devices, or specialized computers, or electronic instruments—will find its revenue plummeting if it can't make any new sales. These companies begin every new year from a base of zero. In order for them to grow, they must first match the prior year and then make incremental sales.

By contrast, a recurring revenue company's starting base isn't zero but last year's level of sales. Because it doesn't have to catch up with last year first, every new sale generates incremental revenue right from the beginning.

A high-tech company without a recurring revenue base probably won't find it too difficult to achieve rapid growth as long as its product is still very early in its life cycle. At this point, market saturation and competition have not yet become problems. But growth certainly gets more difficult every year as the product matures, and new competitors—possibly with better technology—are attracted to the marketplace. Eventually the company will be forced to either develop or acquire new products, if it wants to keep its growth close to the rate it has achieved in the past.

By contrast, the recurring revenue company can keep growing by simply continuing what it has already done successfully in the past. Unless it sets a growth target that is unrealistically high, it's very unlikely that its business will get out of control. This is the kind of emerging growth company that is the most manageable and therefore the most likely to actually deliver good earnings growth consistently. And in my experience, it's also the kind that usually entails the least fundamental risk for the investor.

NEW PRODUCT DEPENDENCE

New products are vitally important to our economy. Without them there would be much less growth and far fewer emerging growth companies. After all, hundreds of emerging growth companies have been started only because the founder couldn't get his original employer to support an innovative new product idea. The only way to turn his dream into reality was to do it himself. So I would no sooner knock new products than I would motherhood or apple pie.

Nevertheless, I don't like companies that are heavily dependent on new products. Hundreds of small companies have stopped growing because they were never able to come up with a follow-on product. In fact, emerging growth companies that are able to develop a successful second product are very unusual. So companies that are heavily dependent on new products tend to be very risky, and I believe it's wise to avoid betting on them. But recurring revenue companies never fall into this category. By their nature there is no reason for them to ever become dangerously dependent on the successful introduction of a new product.

In the case of Hogan Systems, we've already seen what happened to one company whose growth was critically dependent on a new product. Although Hogan's problems were extreme because the Loans System's shortcomings also affected the base of already-existing business, premature introduction of new products has caused severe problems for many emerging growth companies, especially in the technology sector. What usually happens is that the sales force, with plenty of encouragement from management, develops so much enthusiasm for the new product that they neglect the old one. They see the new product as the key that will get them into new accounts that so far have been impossible to crack. They also envision it as something that will be easy to sell to the existing customer base and will be helpful in keeping competitors from encroaching on their territory. So, naturally they can't wait to start selling it.

When the salesforce does start selling a product before it's actually available, the result is almost always disaster. Very often minor manufacturing problems or design bugs delay the product's availability. If the salesmen have neglected the older product line in the meantime, many prospective customers will simply decide to wait for the new one. So sales dry up, and there is only one direction for earnings to go.

Another common problem with new products is that they often require opening up new distribution channels. Most emerging growth companies go from using distributors to developing their own direct sales force, but sometimes the transition works in the opposite direction. This was true in the case of Chyron, a small high-tech company. Chyron's difficulties in developing a network of dealers to handle a new product were largely responsible for bringing its fine record of consistent growth to an end. The company's basic product line is a series of character generators, which television broadcasters use for special video effects. Chyron is so dominant in this market niche that its name has become a generic term, much the way "xerox" is used in reference to any kind of photocopier. At first Chyron's major market was the television networks. When this segment approached saturation, Chyron extended its growth by convincing more and more local stations to use its equipment for their own newscasts. Because Chyron's product was expensive and targeted at a relatively small number of sophisticated users, a direct sales force was the logical choice of distribution channels.

As long as it was able to continue penetrating the local station segment of the market, Chyron grew like clockwork. Each year at the annual meeting the chairman would announce his earnings forecast, and each year the company would beat it by a penny or two. At the same time its profitability was excellent, so it was able to maintain an impeccable balance sheet. However, management realized that saturation would eventually pose a problem in maintaining the historic growth rate. It prepared for the eventual slowdown by developing a stripped-down version of its basic product, which it planned to sell to the non-broadcast market. Potential customers included schools, hotels, hospitals, racetracks, and corporate users. But the company realized it would be impossible to market the new product through its direct sales force. The breadth of the new market and the much lower product price combined to create a different set of economics that ruled that out as an option. Chyron's only choice was to sell the new product through distributors who specialized in commercial audio/video products.

Unfortunately, developing this network turned out to be extremely difficult. Most of the distributors Chyron signed up considered their other lines more important, so they never gave the Chyron product much attention. Then quality-control problems with the initial shipments eroded what little dealer support there was. As a result, the first year's sales fell way short of budget, and the new product line lost money. Instead of alleviating the saturation problem, the new product only exacerbated it. Needless to say, the stock did not do well.

Recurring revenue companies seldom encounter problems like these. With a solid base of business they can count on year after year, they never have to bet so heavily on the successful introduction of a new product.

MATURING GRACEFULLY

Still another significant advantage that recurring revenue companies have over other types of businesses is the ease with which they can mature

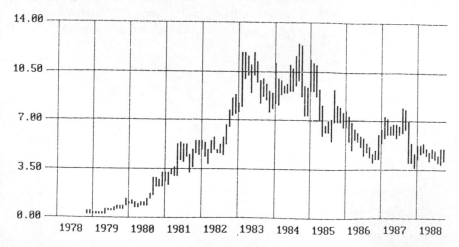

Figure 5.1. Chyron Corporation stock chart. Courtesy of Bridge Information Systems, Inc.

gracefully into healthy cash generators. Cable television is an excellent example of this important characteristic. When a cable company first goes into a new market, it must make heavy front-end investments in equipment and installation. Many of these capital expenditures have to be made before any subscribers can be hooked up and before any revenue can be generated. So for the first year or two of operation, depreciation and interest expense is very high as a percentage of the system's revenue, and it operates at a loss. But these items don't increase very much as more and more new subscribers are added. Therefore, as the system is built out, profit margins rise, and cash flow turns positive. This happens because each additional subscriber generates incremental revenue that is high relative to the extra cost and the extra investment required to tie him into the system.

As the system eventually approaches saturation, revenue growth will taper off substantially, but profit margins will continue to expand, and capital requirements will remain low. Therefore, the business will produce a positive cash flow that grows larger and larger every year. The surplus cash can be paid out to shareholders in the form of dividends; or it can be used to pay down the debt that was probably used to finance the system in the early days, when its cash flow was negative. But no matter what use the cash is put to, the business will have matured gracefully from a financial point of view, and along the way its value is likely to have increased substantially.

Table 5.1 demonstrates what the economics of a typical cable system look like. In the first two years, when revenue growth is highest, the system has a negative net cash flow. By the sixth year it's getting close to maximum penetration, and the rate of revenue growth has dropped all the way down to about 10%. But the business is throwing off plenty of surplus cash because the pretax margin has increased, and there is almost no need to make further capital expenditures.

THE EARNINGS CUSHION

To summarize our discussion so far, a recurring revenue base makes a high-growth business more controllable and easier to run by providing several important advantages:

- More accurate forecasting and control.
- Cookie-cutter simplicity of operations.
- Every year starts from a base well above zero.

TABLE 5.1 Economics of a Typical Cable TV System ($ Million)

Year	1	2	3	4	5	6
Subscribers (000s)						
Start	0	50	100	150	180	200
End	50	100	150	180	200	220
Average	25	75	125	165	190	210
Revenue @ $240/Subscriber	$6.0	$18.0	$30.0	$39.6	$45.6	$50.4
Percentage Change	N/A	200%	66.7%	32%	15.2%	10.5%
Operating Expense	4.0	9.0	14.0	17.0	18.0	19.0
Interest Expense	6.0	7.0	8.0	8.0	8.0	8.0
Depreciation Expense	7.0	8.5	9.0	9.5	10.0	10.5
Pretax Profit	(11.0)	(6.5)	(1.0)	5.1	9.6	12.9
Pretax Margin	Neg.	Neg.	Neg.	12.9%	21.1%	25.6%
Capital Expenditures	70.0	15.0	5.0	5.0	5.0	5.0
Net Cash Flow	(74.0)	(13.0)	3.0	9.6	14.6	18.4

Note: Net cash flow = pretax profit + depreciation expense − capital expenditures

- Little dependence on new products.
- Graceful maturation from a financial perspective.

These characteristics ease the burden on management and reduce the likelihood of a significant earnings shortfall. But recurring revenue also lowers investment risk in a more direct way: by providing an earnings cushion. For example, if a company is expected to earn $1.00 per share, with $.80 of the total coming from a recurring revenue source, only $.20 is left at risk. The company may be counting on a new product, or maybe even an acquisition to supply this $.20. Now let's say these sources don't develop as expected, and there is a 50% shortfall in their contribution. Total earnings would still come in at around $.90 because of the cushioning effect of the recurring revenue part of the business. There may be some investor disappointment with these results, but it won't be severe.

If the earnings proportions are reversed, however, so that just $.20 of the expected $1.00 comes from the recurring revenue part of the business, the outcome is considerably different. With $.80 of earnings at risk, a 50% shortfall causes total earnings to come in at just $.60 per share. You probably don't have to be told that owning stock in an emerging growth company whose earnings come in this far below expectations is neither a pleasant nor a rewarding experience.

So recurring revenue puts a limit on downside earnings risk at the same time it makes a company more controllable and easier to manage. It isn't an absolute guarantee of success—some companies will still find a way to get in trouble. But it does go a long way toward improving the odds. Therefore, I strongly recommend that you weight your portfolio heavily with these high-visibility companies. It's one of the most important steps you can take to make sure your portfolio has the earnings growth that's a prerequisite for good performance.

For an institutional investor, size constraints make it difficult to own nothing but high-visibility companies. But not for individual investors; it's an area where they have an important edge. In the next chapter, we'll take an in-depth look at how the benefits of recurring revenue helped make one of these companies a particularly rewarding investment for its shareholders.

6

Spectradyne: Anatomy of a Winner

Spectradyne was one of the most rewarding stocks any emerging growth investor could have owned in recent years. As I got to know this company well and came to appreciate its many positive attributes, I gradually built up the size of my position. Fortunately, it had become one of my largest holdings by the time it was "put into play" and eventually taken private by a leveraged buy-out partnership that included the company's management, the Bass brothers, and a few other investors. The buy-out occurred at a premium of more than 100% to where the stock had been trading just prior to the first tender offer. But even before this premium was reflected in the price of the stock, Spectradyne had been an excellent long-term investment because of its strong earnings growth.

Even though Spectradyne is no longer a public company, it's well worth analyzing because it has so many of the qualities that you should look for in an emerging growth investment. It's in a relatively simple and straightforward service business whose economics make sense. It has the advantage of a well-entrenched competitive position in a market that's far from saturated. And most important of all, Spectradyne's solid base of recurring revenue provides excellent visibility as well as plenty of cash for reinvestment in future growth. The company also happened to have good management, but its fine growth record was first and foremost attributable to its very favorable business characteristics. These are what made it a winner. They're the same characteristics you should look for in other emerging growth companies as you go through the stock selection process.

I first became aware of Spectradyne because, as a securities analyst, I traveled a lot, frequently visiting companies and attending conferences. Many of the hotels I stayed in offered Spectradyne's in-room, pay-per-view movie system. To watch one of these movies, all you have to do is turn the television to a preset dial, and then make your selection via a small box located on top of the set. This box, which is called a converter, is electronically connected to a central video cassette player and a minicomputer that automatically charges your room bill for each movie.

Spectravision, as the service is known, is wired into about half a million rooms in more than 1,000 hotels—including the Hyatt, Hilton, Marriott, and Sheraton chains. On average just over 12% of the guests occupying a room actually watch a movie. Selections are always quite current since the movie distributors release films to Spectradyne before they become available on cable or cassette. The choices are oriented toward pure entertainment, usually featuring comedy or action. *Top Gun* is a typical Spectradyne offering; *A Passage to India* is not. Some of the late evening selections are clearly geared toward mature audiences, but the company does not show X-rated films.

A primary reason for Spectradyne's growth is that its service benefits all three of the parties involved—the guest, the hotel, and the movie company. A typical viewer is a traveling businessman who is likely to find himself tired, bored, and alone at the end of a long day on the road. Spectravision offers him a convenient way of relaxing with good entertainment that he can enjoy without having to leave his room. Because the movie charge goes directly onto the room bill, 9 times out of 10 it will also end up on his expense account. By eliminating cost as a big consideration in deciding whether or not to watch a movie, this has helped to keep viewing levels high and has prevented free-to-the-guest movies on cable channels from having much impact on Spectravision.

The hotels that offer Spectradyne's service consider it a nice source of extra revenue. Although it's quite small in relation to their total business, it comes very close to being pure profit. And in the competition to attract guests, the service may provide a small edge. Availability of Spectravision is certainly not the first thing you're likely to consider in choosing a hotel, but if you're used to it, you may keep going back to a hotel that offers it.

For the movie distributors, like the hotel chains, Spectradyne represents a good source of incremental profit. It enables them to reach a larger audience than is possible through theaters alone. So the movie distributors, like the hotels, are essential allies who support Spectradyne because it enhances their own profitability.

THE RECURRING REVENUE BASE

One of the key attributes that helped make Spectradyne a winner was its recurring revenue base. The high cost of installing the system limits Spectradyne's market to those hotels that have 300 or more rooms. Even then, the average cost per room exceeds $200. To protect this investment, the company deals only with hotels that agree to a 5-year term contract. These contracts, which are usually renewed or extended with little difficulty, provide the base for Spectradyne's recurring revenue stream and also protect it from direct competition.

Like any company with a substantial amount of recurring revenue, Spectradyne doesn't begin every new year from a starting base of zero but rather from a base that's close to the prior year's level of sales. Therefore, it can show healthy growth even in a year when it produces and sells fewer new units than it did in the prior year. It's difficult to overemphasize just what an extraordinarily attractive business characteristic this is. It provides two important advantages. First, it shields Spectradyne from the usual pressure to develop or acquire new products. It doesn't have to contend with this obstacle that trips up so many small companies. Second, the recurring revenue base enables Spectradyne to routinely make budgets and forecasts that are quite accurate. Its overhead would never get out of control the way Zycad's did. To fully appreciate how these advantages—good visibility and immunity from pressure to develop or acquire new products—have helped Spectradyne achieve rapid, controlled growth, let's take a closer look at the dynamics of its business. The relevant data, either taken directly or derived from annual reports, is shown in Table 6.1.

TABLE 6.1 Spectravision Revenue Growth

	1982	1983	1984	1985	1986
Rooms (000s)					
Beginning	123.1	160.7	200.1	258.1	306.9
Net Increase	37.6	39.4	58.0	48.8	64.7
End	160.7	200.1	258.1	306.9	371.6
Average	141.9	180.4	229.1	282.5	339.3
Occupancy	67.6%	68.0%	68.0%	65.7%	65.3%
Viewing Level	12.2%	12.7%	11.6%	12.6%	12.6%
Average Price	$5.03	$5.23	$5.72	$5.79	$5.91
Revenue ($ millions)	$21.5	$29.8	$37.8	$49.4	$60.3
Percentage Increase	30.3%	38.4%	27.1%	30.5%	22.1%
Percentage Increase—Average Rooms	31.2%	27.1%	27.0%	23.3%	20.1%

Spectradyne's pay-per-view business is best analyzed in terms of four variables that control it:

1. The average number of hotel rooms offering the service.
2. The occupancy rate of the rooms.
3. The viewing level per occupied room.
4. The average price per movie.

These four numbers multiplied out and then multiplied by the number of days in the year equal total revenue.

Over the 5-year period shown in the table, both occupancy and viewing levels have experienced only very minor year-to-year fluctuations. And the average price (which is a derived number and therefore contains rounding errors) increased significantly only in one year, 1984. Therefore, the average number of rooms is left as far and away the most important variable for determining the company's growth. You can see that in 1982, 1984, and 1986, the rate of revenue growth was extremely close to the increase in the average number of rooms. In the other 2 years, 1983 and 1985, revenue grew faster than the room base, primarily because the viewing level increased from the preceding year. So if history is an accurate guide to the future, Spectradyne's pay-per-view revenue will continue to grow at least as fast as the rate at which the room base expands.

By analyzing the historic data, we can focus in on several important characteristics of Spectradyne's business. Let's start by making the unrealistic assumption that in 1987 the company was completely unsuccessful in selling its service to any new hotels, so for the year there was no net change in the number of rooms. In this case, the average rooms for the year would have been 371,600, exactly the same as the 1986 *year-end* number. Even though there would have been no growth from this level, the average number of rooms for the *full year* would still have increased by nearly 10%. And in light of what we know about Spectradyne's past growth, it would be reasonable to expect revenue to have also grown at about a 10% rate.

By comparison, if this same zero sales assumption is applied to a typical manufacturing company that has no base of recurring revenue, the result is more than a little bit different: Revenue falls all the way to zero. The underlying assumption may be extreme, but the dramatic contrast in results shows just how big an advantage it is for a company to have a recurring revenue base.

Now let's make a more realistic assumption as to how many rooms Spectradyne might be able to add to its base. A good conservative estimate would be 65,000, the same number it actually installed in the prior year. Because it has already done this many, we can be confident the necessary manufacturing capacity, sales force, and field service organization are already in place. The addition of 65,000 new rooms means an increase in the base of about 19%. And given what we know about Spectradyne's growth dynamics, the revenue increase ought to at least match that rate. So by merely repeating in cookie-cutter fashion no more than what it has already done in the preceding year, Spectradyne should be able to grow at 19% or better. As you can see, the recurring revenue base makes it relatively easy for the company to prolong its growth.

Eventually, however, the rate of revenue growth will taper off. Every year as the size of the room base expands, Spectradyne will move closer to saturation, and it will become harder and harder to maintain a constant rate of growth. This obviously raises the question of what other sources of growth might be available, but it also has some important financial implications that we should consider first.

MATURING GRACEFULLY

Because of its large base of recurring revenue, Spectradyne is in an excellent position to mature gracefully from a financial perspective. To understand why, let's look at the trends in its cash flow and capital spending, shown in Table 6.2. The most striking aspect of Spectradyne's finances is the heavy depreciation charges that make cash flow so much greater than net income. For instance, in 1986 total cash flow of $22.9 million was more than $3 \times$ higher than net income of $6.9 million. A ratio this high reflects the fact that Spectradyne's business is capital intensive. Like a cable TV company, its recurring revenue stream doesn't begin to flow until a sizable front-end investment has been made.

During the 5 years shown in Table 6.2, Spectradyne's depreciation and cash flow actually grew quite a bit faster than its net income. This was

TABLE 6.2 Spectradyne Cash Flow Summary

	1982	1983	1984	1985	1986
Cash Flow from Operations ($ million)					
Net Income	$2.7	$3.8	$4.7	$6.5	$6.9
Depreciation	3.6	5.3	8.9	14.5	18.3
Other Sources	.2	(2.9)	3.2	—	(2.3)
Total	6.5	6.2	16.8	21.0	22.9
Cost of Systems Installed	7.6	14.0	25.0	25.5	29.9
Cash Flow Surplus/(Shortfall)	(1.1)	(7.8)	(8.2)	(4.5)	(7.0)

primarily because of an accounting change made early in the period. By adopting a more conservative depreciation policy, which had no effect on total cash flow, the company increased depreciation expense and decreased net income. Elimination of the investment tax credit in 1986 also had a negative impact on net income but didn't affect the depreciation component of cash flow.

Although Spectradyne's cash flow grew rapidly during this period, it never matched the amount spent on wiring new rooms. The company had to rely on bank borrowings and occasional equity offerings to finance this shortfall. But in the future, when Spectradyne's growth rate tapers off, it will become less dependent on external capital, and eventually it will even generate large cash surpluses. To understand why this will happen, let's again make the extreme assumption that growth came to a screeching halt in 1987 and no new rooms were added to the base. In that case, the net cash flow from operations would have increased to about $26 million. And because no new systems were being installed, capital spending would theoretically have dropped all the way from $29.9 million to zero. Suddenly the company's perennial cash flow shortfall would have turned into a surplus of $26 million. Moreover, this surplus would be generated year after year because of the recurring nature of the revenue stream.

Of course, in reality, Spectradyne's growth won't come to such an abrupt halt but will taper off gradually. When the annual room additions eventually decline, capital spending will also turn down. But the cash flow generated from operations will continue to grow. As shown in Figure 6.1, the two lines will eventually cross, and at that point Spectradyne will turn into a net cash generator. And as we go further out in time, capital spending will decline even more, and the cash flow from operations will keep on growing. So every year the company will generate more and more surplus cash that can either be reinvested in other business areas or be paid out to the shareholders. But no matter how this surplus is used, the company will have matured gracefully into a healthy cash cow.

GROWTH OPPORTUNITIES FROM APPLIED TECHNOLOGY

What will Spectradyne actually do with the surplus cash that its pay-per-view business is bound to eventually throw off? Now that it's private, most of the cash flow will probably be used to pay down the debt that was used to finance the leveraged buy-out. But when it was a public company, one of the things that made Spectradyne so attractive was its abundance of reinvestment opportunities. These opportunities existed because Spectradyne is an applied technology company that can leverage off its base of

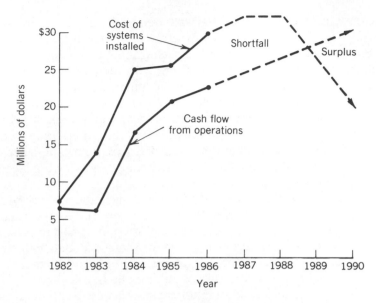

Figure 6.1. Spectradyne cash flow and capital spending.

installed systems to create further growth. To understand how this is possible, it's useful to think of the systems Spectradyne wires into hotels as more than just a means of transmitting movies. In effect, they are also electronic communications networks that link a central computer to each guest room. In these networks the guest's movie selection is just one form of input; the movie he receives back is just one form of output. With some software modifications, these same networks can be used to send other types of information back and forth.

As an applied technology company dealing in electronic communications, Spectradyne is a direct beneficiary of the semiconductor industry's constant flow of price/performance improvements. The same advances in semiconductor technology that have made it possible for today's desk-top computers to surpass the power of yesterday's mainframes have also enabled Spectradyne to rev up the power of its systems, opening up new avenues of growth. For instance, in the mid-1980s the company took advantage of cheaper and more powerful semiconductors as building blocks with which to design and manufacture a vastly improved converter. The new converter incorporated a huge increase in channel capacity; 60 channels were now available compared to just 4 with the old version. This paved the way for a number of new services that have become important revenue generators.

The first of the new services was free-to-the-guest entertainment, which consists of several channels of cable programming such as ESPN, Home Box Office, and Cable News. Spectradyne buys this programming and transmits it through its system, along with the pay-per-view movies. Many hotels like to offer it as an additional amenity and pay Spectradyne a flat monthly fee, unrelated to occupancy, to receive it. By 1986, only the fourth year it was offered, free-to-the-guest service accounted for just over $13 million of revenue—17% of Spectradyne's total. In addition to the incremental revenue, it also enhanced the stability of the business because it isn't subject to the fluctuations in hotel occupancy and viewing levels that affect pay-per-view revenue.

You might think that Spectradyne risked harming its pay-per-view business when it introduced free-to-the-guest service. At the time, this was a common concern among institutional investors, and it caused one prominent analyst to turn quite negative on the stock. But the company did a lot of careful testing before it committed itself, and it correctly predicted that its pay-per-view business would not be cannibalized.

Actually the expansion of channel capacity had a positive impact on the viewing level that more than offset any loss from free-to-the-guest programming. With the additional capacity, it became possible to offer a preview channel, and even more important, a greater selection of movies. As a result of these improvements, viewing levels increased to an average of 12.4% in 1983–1986, up from 11.8% in the 3 years preceding introduction of the 60-channel system.

This increase in the viewing level was particularly significant because of Spectradyne's cost structure. When one extra guest decides to watch a movie on Spectravision, there is very little additional cost incurred. The royalties paid to the movie distributor and the hotel increase, but that's all. The other costs are fixed. So about 75% to 80% of the incremental revenue from higher viewing flows through to pretax profit.

A company with this kind of cost structure is said to have a high degree of operating leverage; a small change in its unit volume translates into a big change in is profits. For instance, in 1986 when Spectradyne earned $.72 per share, an increase of just 0.5% in the viewing level would have added $.10 to its earnings. Of course, operating leverage is a double-edged sword. And over the years, dips in the viewing level occasionally caused Spectradyne to report unfavorable quarterly earnings comparisons.

OTHER NEW SERVICES

Another benefit of expanded channel capacity was that it made possible several completely new services. Foremost among these is an in-room checkout system that uses the television set as a monitor and makes it possible for the guest to review his bill prior to checking out. If the charges are correct, he can just approve the bill and pick up a hard copy without having to wait in the checkout line. Other services of this type—message retrieval, room status reporting, and room service breakfast menu—have also been introduced recently.

The revenue generated by these new services, even in combination, may never match that of pay-per-view movies. But they are very profitable pieces of business because they require almost no new investment; the hardware is already in place. However, the benefit of the new services extends beyond their profit contribution. They've also helped Spectradyne to become a more important supplier to the hotel industry. This has made it easier to sell the basic pay-per-view system to new hotels and has provided added leverage for negotiating contract renewals with existing hotels.

EXPANDING THE PAY-PER-VIEW BUSINESS

Although new electronic technology has already made it possible for Spectradyne to offer several important new services, its greatest impact by far may be expansion of the already-existing market for pay-per-view movies. At the time Spectradyne was bought out, it had installed its system only in hotels larger than 300 rooms; the cost was too high to allow an acceptable return on investment in smaller hotels. There were approximately 1.1 million rooms that met this minimum size cutoff, and of these about 800,000 were probably legitimate candidates. So the company had penetrated about 50% of its potential market.

But as cheaper and more powerful semiconductors become available, Spectradyne should eventually be able to design a low-cost version of its system specifically targeted at hotels in the 200- to 300-room-size range. If it can serve this segment of the market profitably, it will double the number of rooms it hasn't yet penetrated and add at least several more years of growth to its pay-per-view business.

AN ATYPICAL TECHNOLOGY COMPANY

New technology has obviously been an important contributor to Spectradyne's growth. It has paved the way for the development of new services, higher viewing levels, and expansion of the base business' potential market. But Spectradyne is quite unlike most technology companies and was seldom thought of as being part of that group. In fact, at investor conferences sponsored by the American Electronics Association, many analysts and portfolio managers shunned Spectradyne because it wasn't high-tech enough for them.

One thing that sets Spectradyne apart is that, instead of developing new technology and selling it to others, Spectradyne takes technology that other companies have developed and applies it to its own business. So it benefits from the research and development efforts of other companies without sharing the risk. Another distinction is that new products and services are important to Spectradyne, but certainly not critical. They may add 5% or 10% to its growth rate, but it can still grow without them. So, as a public company, Spectradyne was never under any severe pressure to risk bringing them to market prematurely. This is in sharp contrast to the typical technology company whose competitive position and growth rate may be riding completely on the timing and market acceptance of its new product introductions. Spectradyne never would have experienced a problem like the one Hogan Systems created for itself when it rushed its Loans System to market prematurely.

WEAKNESSES

In spite of all its very favorable business characteristics, like any other company, Spectradyne also has some weaknesses that should be considered to keep the discussion in perspective. The most serious is its dependence on the hotel chains. Although Spectradyne adds to the hotels' profits, its contribution isn't large enough to give it much influence with them. For instance, some hotels have forced it to show tamer late night selections than it would prefer. Because these movies are by far the most profitable, the impact is noticeable. The company's management certainly recognizes this vulnerability and has tried to lessen it. New services like in-room checkout have helped strengthen its position as a supplier to the hotel industry, but Spectradyne will always need the hotels more than they need it.

The operating leverage we discussed earlier is responsible for another weakness—one that was particularly important when Spectradyne was a public company. As a result of its high fixed costs, earnings were very sensitive to changes in the viewing level. This was especially noticeable on a quarterly basis. For example, viewing took a sharp drop during the 1984 Summer Olympics, and Spectradyne reported lower earnings for that quarter. By contrast, operating leverage had a favorable effect in the first quarter of 1987 because *Top Gun*, which shattered all viewing records, was shown during that period. These quarterly fluctuations make little difference to Spectradyne now that it's private, but when it was a public company they probably put downward pressure on its P/E ratio. And they certainly caused investors some anxiety.

STOCK PERFORMANCE

Now that we understand what made Spectradyne tick as a company, let's turn to analyzing it as a stock market investment. In May 1987, Marvin Davis, the oilman turned movie mogul, "put the company in play" when he announced a $37-per-share cash tender offer. Davis's offer seemed generous, but a few weeks later another group of investors that included management and the Bass brothers offered a package of cash and securities valued at $46 per share. This price represented more than a double from where the stock had traded earlier in the year. And less than 3 years before, it had sold as low as $6. So Spectradyne provided a very high return, even to a long-term investor who was unlucky enough to have sold it just before the buy-out.

Tender offers always come at a premium to the market, but this one was particularly large because the private buyers valued the company on a much different basis than public stock market investors had. At the time of the offer, most analysts were projecting that earnings would be in a range of $.90 to $1.00 for the full year. Selling in the low 20s, the stock appeared to be fairly priced by the conventional yardstick of an earnings multiple. But the private buyers were valuing it on a multiple of *cash flow, not earnings.* They recognized that Spectradyne had a lot of characteristics in common with cable TV companies and that it made sense to value it on the same basis.

Cable TV systems are effectively monopolies because of the heavy front-end investment. It would be suicidal for a new competitor to enter a market already served by an existing system. Although the high capital requirements keep out competition, they also depress reported earnings because depreciation charges are so high relative to revenue. Private market buyers recognize this, so transaction prices are based on a multiple of cash flow rather than earnings.

Like a cable TV company, Spectradyne's cash flow was also much higher than reported earnings because of heavy depreciation charges. The $46 tender offer was actually very much in line with the cash flow multiples being paid in private purchases of cable TV systems. On this basis, the offer looked about right, even though the buyers appeared to be overpaying by a lot in terms of a multiple of reported earnings.

Long-term investors who understood Spectradyne realized it had much in common with the cable TV business and recognized the possibility that it could eventually sell at a multiple of cash flow rather than earnings. Knowing the gap between public and private valuations might someday be closed, they had the patience to hold the stock through periods of apparent overvaluation and through periods when quarterly earnings comparisons were below average. In the end, their patience was rewarded by a valuation premium that turned a good investment into a great one.

WHAT MADE IT A WINNER

Because Spectradyne is no longer a public company and therefore no longer a potential candidate for investment, the amount of time we have spent discussing it may seem excessive. However, other companies have the same characteristics that made it such a great stock. As an emerging growth investor, your challenge is to find them.

Spectradyne was a rewarding investment because of four key reasons:

1. The recurring revenue base enabled management to grow the company rapidly and still keep it under control.
2. Spectradyne's ability to leverage off an existing asset—its installed base of systems—facilitated its growth.
3. As an applied technology company, Spectradyne benefited from the research and development efforts of other companies without incurring the risk.
4. There was a substantial gap between the public market price and the valuation that private investors were willing to pay for the company.

Of course, there was no way of knowing for sure if the last factor would ever come into play. But it was certainly possible to recognize the first three ahead of time, and they provided plenty of reason to own the stock. The buy-out was just the icing on the cake.

7

Why the Odds Favor
Service Companies

Companies that have good visibility and a high level of recurring revenue are most often in service, rather than manufacturing businesses. And many service companies have other qualities that also make them more manageable and therefore less susceptible to earnings shortfalls. So as you search for good emerging growth investments, you will do well to be particularly alert for service companies.

By definition, service companies are close to their customers. Therefore, they don't have to contend with long distribution channels and inventory cycles—two problems that can really increase the difficulty of keeping a fast-growing business under control. And being close to their customers usually allows service companies to compete on more than the basis of price alone. Convenience, reliability, and support are frequently more important to the customer.

For example, consider a small bank that realizes an outside facilities management company should be brought in to run its data-processing operations. Even though the need may be obvious, actually hiring a service company to take over this function is a decision the bank won't make lightly. Data processing is a vitally important part of any bank's business. Turning it over to a company that fails to do the job accurately and on time will disrupt operations completely and could even put the bank's survival at risk. So there is no way the decision will be made until the bank is fully convinced of the service company's reliability. Before committing itself, the bank will check out each company thoroughly. And once a choice has been made, that company will be very hard to displace as long as it continues to provide good, reliable service. Throughout the entire decision process, reliability is the primary consideration; price is strictly secondary in importance.

By contrast, manufactured products often become commodity-like as they mature, so price is left as the only criterion customers have to distinguish one competitor from another. When this happens, the manufacturer with the lowest cost structure has a great advantage. Just consider the industries where U.S. companies have been hurt so badly by foreign competitors. Steel, automobiles, consumer electronics, and the like are all manufacturing rather than service businesses.

HOME OFFICE REFERENCE LABORATORY

To get a better feel for some of the differences between service and manufacturing businesses, let's look at Home Office Reference Laboratory, Inc.—a company with some attractive characteristics often associated with service companies. This company is the nation's largest provider of laboratory testing services to the life insurance industry. Throughout its 16-year history, it has focused on just this one market niche. Although there are hundreds of other commercial laboratories that provide similar services to hospitals and physicians, HORL has very few competitors that specialize in testing for the insurance industry. As a result, it has developed a client base that includes over 800 life insurance companies, and it has established an industry reputation for prompt delivery of accurate test results on a cost-effective basis.

The tests performed by HORL are specifically designed to help life insurance companies assess the mortality risk of a person applying for a policy. For instance, they measure cholesterol levels, glucose levels associated with diabetic risk, and data indicative of alcoholic liver disease. The tests also detect the presence of certain prescription drugs (beta blockers, for instance), which mask the symptoms of cardiovascular and other disorders and make them more difficult to detect by a physical examination. And the company has a proprietary process for measuring the presence of nicotine in a urine specimen. This is important to life insurers because premium rates are affected by whether or not the applicant is a smoker.

In 1985 HORL introduced two very important new services: a test for cocaine and other controlled substances, and an AIDS-related test. As shown in Table 7.1, these have had extraordinary acceptance and have been responsible for much of the company's explosive growth. From the

TABLE 7.1 Home Office Reference Laboratory, Inc. ($000s)

Year	1985	1986	1987
Revenue			
Urinalyses	$ 6,279	$ 7,219	$ 9,247
Blood Chemistry Profiles	2,275	4,089	12,404
Controlled Substance Profiles	38	1,073	4,718
AIDS-Related Tests	122	2,012	8,630
Other Operations	1,834	2,133	4,147
Total Revenue	$10,548	$16,522	$39,146
Net Income	$ 1,442	$ 3,088	$12,435
Earnings per Share	$.10	$.21	$.83
Cash Flow from Operations	$2,699	$4,460	$14,293
Cash Required for Increased Working Capital	128	802	3,972
Investment in Property, Plant, and Equipment	459	1,074	9,979
Surplus	$2,112	$2,584	$ 342

life insurance industry's perspective, the significant thing about AIDS and cocaine abuse isn't just their obvious impact on mortality but also the fact that they primarily affect people in the 20 to 49 age group, which is otherwise a low-risk category. Because of these new threats, insurers have been dropping the policy size threshold at which they test. Until recently, almost all tests were conducted for policies above $300,000—only 2% of the total number of new policies written. However, the threshold has been rapidly coming down toward the $100,000 level, which encompasses 24% of all policies. This would represent a 12-fold increase in the size of the available market.

Obviously HORL operates in an industry environment that has been extremely fertile for high growth. Although this has attracted increased competition, as a service company, HORL has some important advantages that will help it meet this threat. By focusing exclusively on the insurance industry as its only customer base, it has developed very close working relationships with its clients. Over the years, it has helped them with a number of specific problems. For instance, the nicotine test was custom designed for insurance use. And the company has developed a management information system specifically tailored to help it meet the needs of its clients, all of whom have slightly different testing requirements according to the size of the policy, the applicant's age, geographic location, and other considerations. This system is essential for providing quick, efficient responses to a wide variety of testing requirements. With it, HORL is able to report test results within 24 hours by virtually any means the client specifies, including computer-to-computer data transmission. All of this has contributed to the company's reputation for responsiveness, service, and reliability—factors that are very important to the clients. If it had to compete solely on the basis of price, its margins would be much more vulnerable to downward pressure.

A remarkable aspect of HORL's financial performance is that, in spite of its very rapid growth, it has been able to finance all of its capital expenditures and increased working capital requirements out of its cash flow from operations. If it were a manufacturing company, it undoubtedly would have had to take down debt or resorted to a dilutive equity offering. But two important characteristics have allowed it to self-finance its growth. First, its high margins provide a lot of earnings that can be ploughed back into the business. Second, it is not capital-intensive. Like many service companies, HORL does not need a lot of assets to generate revenue. Its business doesn't require expensive investments in manufacturing plants. And it's able to operate without much inventory, other than a few supplies. This also keeps it from being capital-intensive. But even more important, the lack of inventory requirements frees the company from having to contend with inventory cycles. Like long sales cycles, inventory cycles can really increase the complexity of a business and make it more difficult to control. Naturally, manufacturing companies can't operate without inventory, but it's a significant advantage that many service companies enjoy.

INVENTORY CYCLES

Inventory cycles are important to understand because they can cause surprising volatility in what would otherwise appear to be a reasonably stable business. This volatility occurs when all the companies involved in the manufacturing, distribution, and sale of a product adjust their inventory levels in response to a small change in end demand. As the change works its way through the system, its effect is magnified.

Table 7.2 illustrates how an inventory cycle works. In this example there are just three participants in the distribution channel. From left to right, there is first the retailer (Column 1), who buys product from a distributor (Column 2), who in turn purchases from a manufacturer (Column 3). All three like to keep their inventory 20% above the amount they expect to sell in a month. They make their sales forecasts by simply assuming that this month's sales will be equal to last month's. As indicated by the diagonal arrows, the retailer's purchases determine the distributor's sales, and the distributor's purchases determine the manufacturer's sales.

During the first month, the entire system is in balance—the retailer, the distributor, and the manufacturer all sell 100 units and maintain inven-

TABLE 7.2 A Typical Inventory Cycle

	Retailer	Distributor	Manufacturer
Month 1			
Starting Inventory	120	120	120
Sales	−100	−100	−100
Purchase/Manufacture	+100	+100	+100
Ending Inventory	120	120	120
Month 2			
Starting Inventory	120	120	120
Sales	−96	−100	−100
Purchase/Manufacture	+100	+100	+100
Ending Inventory	124	120	120
Month 3			
Starting Inventory	124	120	120
Sales	−96	−87	−100
Purchase/Manufacture	+87	+100	+100
Ending Inventory	115	133	120
Month 4			
Starting Inventory	115	133	120
Sales	−96	−96	−58
Purchase/Manufacture	+96	+58	+100
Ending Inventory	115	95	162

tory at 120 units. But during the second month, final sales take an unexpected drop of 4 units, leaving the retailer with 124 units of inventory at the end of the month. This represents more than just 4 units of excess inventory because the retailer now expects to sell 96 units instead of 100 in the upcoming month. At this lower level of sales he only needs 115 units of inventory. To get his inventory down to this level he cuts his purchases back from 100 units to 87 units in the third month. This adjustment causes the distributor's sales to drop off by 13 units, and now he has more inventory than he needs. To bring his inventory into line with the lower level of sales he now expects, the distributor must make a larger adjustment than the retailer did. He cuts his purchases from the manufacturer all the way down to 58 units in the fourth month. So what started out as a modest 4% decline in final demand has been magnified into a 42% drop by the time it works its way through the system back to the manufacturing level.

This is a simple model. If you add on to it another layer or two of distribution, plus cyclical and seasonal fluctuations in final demand, you begin to see why inventory cycles are more than a trivial problem for manufacturing companies. They're a problem that service companies don't have to contend with, and when you are trying to keep control of a rapidly growing company, it is very helpful to have as few problems as possible.

SEMICONDUCTORS

Perhaps the best way to appreciate the favorable attributes of service businesses is to examine an industry that has absolutely none of them. For this purpose, there is no better example than the semiconductor industry. With a secular growth rate in excess of 15% and no shortage of entrepreneurial spirit and venture capital backing, there have always been plenty of emerging growth companies in this industry. Yet it has been very difficult for long-term investors to earn good returns with these stocks, primarily because the business is so cyclical and so tough to manage that few semiconductor companies have been able to produce consistent earnings growth.

Some products have what economists refer to as very low elasticity of demand—manufacturers sell about the same quantity regardless of price. A lot of medical products fall into this category. For instance, a company producing artificial heart valves will probably not experience any noticeable increase in unit sales if it cuts its price from $500 to $300. It is absurd to think that someone who needed one of these valves would refuse to pay an extra $200 for it.

Semiconductors are the opposite. Demand for them has proven to be very sensitive to price. As the price of chips has come down, users have designed them into more and more products, causing what industry analysts like to call a pervasion of electronics. This is reflected in the availability of products like digital watches, calculators, and telephones at prices that seem almost ridiculously cheap.

The high elasticity of demand for semiconductors has caused the industry to embrace a strategy called "experience curve pricing." It's based on the idea that as a company manufactures more and more of a particular chip, it gains valuable experience that it can use to fine-tune the production process. This fine tuning results in higher yields and other improvements, which reduce the cost of manufacturing the chips. The cost reductions are then passed on to the customers in the form of lower prices, and this stimulates demand. The higher demand pushes manufacturing still farther out on the experience curve—leading to still more reductions in costs and prices.

The entire process just keeps repeating itself until eventually one manufacturer develops a new generation chip design. The new design crams much more circuitry onto the same-sized silicon wafer and substantially reduces the cost per function from the level of the previous generation.

This encourages more users to incorporate even more chips into the design of their products, so that demand receives another boost. Then the whole process of experience curve pricing starts all over again and continues until yet another generation of new chips is developed.

CYCLICALITY

As you can imagine, any industry that operates under this kind of philosophy is bound to be highly competitive and constantly changing. The dynamics of experience curve pricing have endowed the semiconductor industry with an underlying growth rate in excess of 15%. But this growth has been very cyclical. In part the cyclicality is attributable to the fact that many of the products semiconductors go into—computers and other kinds of high-tech capital goods being particularly noteworthy examples—experience cyclical demand themselves. But this is greatly magnified by the inventory cycles that always affect the industry. Figure 7.1 traces these cycles of semiconductor bookings (orders) and billings (shipments).

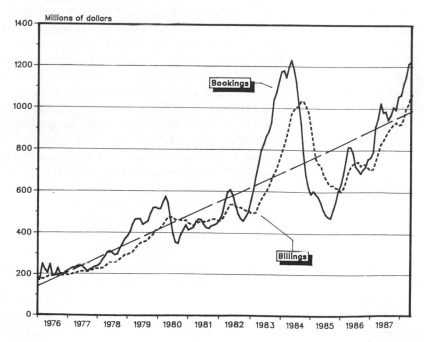

Figure 7.1. U.S. semiconductor bookings and billings (dollars in millions). Courtesy of Andrew Kessler.

One of the industry's most extreme cycles got underway in late 1982 when monthly billings troughed out at slightly less than $500 million, setting the stage for a massive upward movement. Fueled by an expanding economy, burgeoning acceptance of personal computers as a productivity tool in the workplace, and a host of other new high-tech applications, the demand for chips took off like a rocket. In just 18 months, billings more than doubled, eventually reaching a peak of over $1 billion. By the second half of 1983, distributors and users of semiconductors began to worry that this rapid growth would soon lead to shortages. To protect themselves, they attempted to build up their inventories and placed double orders with the manufacturers. The double ordering created backlogs that appeared to be extraordinarily long and further bolstered the confidence of the manufacturers, who were already riding high. Most of them decided to make substantial capacity additions to accomodate the growth they felt confident would continue. Their timing could not have been worse. Shipments were about to fall off a cliff.

By early 1984, a slowdown in demand began to affect many of the technology products that were big users of semiconductors. It seemed that every one of the Fortune 500 companies had been on a buying spree for high-tech equipment, and now suddenly they wanted to catch their breath long enough to figure out what they had bought and how to use it. As the slowdown became apparent, the shortage psychology evaporated faster than a drop of water hitting a hot frying pan. Users and distributors immediately canceled the double orders they had placed earlier and began to work down their inventories, realizing the manufacturers would now be able to supply chips on very short notice. This abrupt change in the willingness of users and distributors to hold inventory greatly magnified the softening of end demand and caused order bookings to plummet over the next year and a half. From peak to trough, bookings took a breathtaking 60% drop. The cycle in actual shipments was somewhat less severe. They only fell about 40%.

DIFFICULT DECISIONS

As they were whipped through the ups and downs of this roller coaster cycle, the semiconductor companies were forced to carry out a very delicate balancing act. Having to choose between the short-term need to maintain their financial integrity versus the desirability of investing in longer term growth opportunities, they faced some extraordinarily difficult decisions. To what extent should you reduce capital spending in an industry that demands productivity increases to remain competitive? Does it make sense to cut back research and development spending when the surest way to improve your competitive position is by being first to bring out a new product? On the other hand, what good is a technology advantage if the downward part of the cycle hits your company so severely that it's left permanently weakened?

There were no easy answers to any of these questions. In fact, the difficulty of the decisions facing the typical semiconductor company made even Zycad and Hogan look like relatively easy businesses to run.

Service companies, especially those with a recurring revenue base, don't have to contend with any of the difficult problems that faced the semiconductor industry. Without inventory cycles to muck up the waters, they have enough visibility to make reasonably accurate forecasts and plan their growth accordingly. They can compete on the basis of support, service, reliability, and convenience—not just price. They don't operate under constant competitive pressure to improve productivity, lower prices, and develop new products. Because they don't need much plant or inventory, their businesses aren't capital-intensive. So most of their growth can be financed with internally generated funds, and they don't have to constantly worry about getting to the equity market while the window is open.

By contrast, the semiconductor industry's business environment is much less benign. Good management and good technology are prerequisites just for survival. A lot of other businesses—particularly service businesses—are much less demanding to run and much easier to keep under control. I believe this also makes them much easier places to make money.

Although I have yet to meet one, there may be a few investors who, through a combination of luck and insight, can do a reasonable job of anticipating semiconductor cycles. But it's a very tough way to make a living. If you're not forced to, why take the added risk of investing in this kind of company? Don't forfeit your selectivity advantage. Instead, keep your portfolio heavily weighted with service companies. They're much more likely to deliver the earnings you need to make the emerging growth style of investing work for you.

8

Home-Run Stocks

Our discussion of stock selection began with the obvious statement that emerging growth investing can work only if the companies in your portfolio actually experience earnings growth that is well above average. We've seen there are a number of basic standards and guidelines that will improve the odds of this happening. To summarize, they include the following:

- Past growth and profitability.
- Industry environment.
- Competition.
- Management.
- Avoiding tough businesses.
- Concentrating on companies with good visibility and recurring revenue.
- Concentrating on noncyclical service companies.

These standards and guidelines will help prevent your portfolio from being creamed by disappointing earnings shortfalls. But all of them are essentially defensive. They'll help you build a portfolio that's like a baseball team that wins because it doesn't give up many runs. These solid defensive teams keep fielding errors and pitching mistakes to a minimum, so they don't have to waste precious runs to catch up with their opponents. Instead, when they score, it's usually to establish a lead or increase one. Likewise, if you keep stock selection mistakes to a minimum, the winners in your portfolio will be able to establish a lead, and you won't always be struggling to come from behind.

However, good defense is only half the game. A few power hitters who can put runs on the scoreboard in a hurry make a huge difference in the number of games a team wins. During the many years he managed the Baltimore Orioles, Earl Weaver never overlooked the importance of offense, and he compiled one of the best long-term records in baseball. Rather than relying on sacrifice bunts, Earl always considered "Dr. Long-ball" a manager's best friend.

And just as most winning baseball teams have a few long-ball hitters on their side, successful emerging growth investors usually own a few big winners—home-run stocks—that really help the performance of their portfolios.

LEVERAGE FACTORS

Home-run stocks nearly always owe their spectacular performance to several factors working in combination. First, their earnings growth isn't just high, it's also above expectations. As a result of these favorable earnings surprises, the stock attracts the attention of more and more investors, who ratchet up their expectations of future growth. As they gradually become willing to pay more for a share of the company, they drive the P/E ratio higher. This P/E expansion, combined with rapid earnings growth, is what creates very high returns. It's like a jet plane switching on the afterburner: If you thought the stock was moving before, just wait a second.

What causes an emerging growth company to show earnings gains that are significantly above estimates? Strong sales growth helps of course, but favorable surprises are usually caused by rising profit margins. In formulating their earnings estimates, securities analysts seldom allow for much benefit from margin expansion. So when margins do increase, investors are often taken by surprise.

The caution typically displayed by analysts isn't difficult to understand. Suppose an analyst projects that a company's sales and earnings will both grow at a 25% rate; the sales projection proves correct, but margin expansion causes earnings to actually increase at a 35% rate. If this happens, none of the analyst's clients will really be unhappy because they already own the stock. But there will be disappointed clients if he is too aggressive in his margin assumption and earnings come in below his estimate. Because the analyst is penalized only for being too aggressive, he has a strong incentive to make conservative forecasts. And because of this bias, expanding margins will usually result in earnings that surprise investors and exceed analysts' estimates.

Here is a profile of how margin expansion can combine with a rising P/E ratio to produce a home-run stock:

Year	Sales	Aftertax Margin	EPS	P/E	Stock Price
1	$20	6%	$1.20	15×	18
2	26	8	2.08		
3	34	10	3.40		
4	44	12	5.28	25×	132
Compound Annual Growth	30%		64%		94%

This hypothetical company's sales grow at a compound annual rate of 30%, which is certainly healthy but not really exceptional considering that the starting base is only $20 million. The aftertax profit margin increases steadily from 6% to 12%, reaching a level that is definitely attainable for any company that has a proprietary product or service and is reasonably well run. But this margin expansion results in very significant leverage: It transforms 30% sales growth into 64% earnings growth.

Then even more leverage occurs as the stock becomes better known and investors' level of confidence in the company increases. They bid the stock's P/E up from 15× to 25× earnings, and this leverages the 64% earnings growth into a 94% compound annual rate of return. In a 4-year period, the value of the original investment grows more than sevenfold. And it doesn't require any outlandish assumptions for this to happen. Stocks like this can do wonders for performance. No one is ever going to have an entire portfolio full of them, but when their returns are so high, just owning one or two makes a big difference.

In this example, the key to spectacular stock performance is the company's margin expansion. If margins hadn't increased, earnings would have grown at the same rate as sales, and there probably would have been no change in the P/E ratio. So the stock's annual return would have been 30% instead of 94%—not bad at all, but not a home-run either.

INDUSTRIES IN TRANSITION

Industries that are experiencing an improvement in their operating environment are one good place to look for emerging growth companies that have potential for margin expansion. The first thing that helps them is higher prices. As demand picks up, more business becomes available to everyone, so pricing turns less competitive, and more costs are passed on to the customer. But this isn't the only factor that leads to higher margins. At first, company managements are naturally skeptical of whether the improvement is for real. Until they become convinced that it's more than a temporary blip, they drag their heels in hiring new employees and expanding physical capacity to accommodate the higher level of demand. As a result of this caution, some cost items—depreciation, interest, and overhead particularly—don't increase as fast as sales. And this leads to further margin expansion.

These are the kind of conditions the oil service industry experienced from 1973 through 1981. For many years prior to then, surplus producing capacity had kept world oil prices flat, and domestic natural gas prices had been regulated at low levels. As a result, U.S. drilling activity stagnated for a long time. That all changed dramatically in 1973 when OPEC took control of world markets and pushed prices significantly higher. Drilling activity entered a long recovery phase, and nearly every company in the oil service business experienced strong demand. Suddenly the industry was short of capacity, and it became easy to raise prices. Margin expansion and strong sales growth combined to produce leveraged earnings gains, and the stocks proved to be very good investments throughout most of this period. More recently, companies involved in waste disposal and environmental cleanup have experienced a similar kind of improvement, as both government and private industry have increased their spending in this area.

FAVORABLE COST STRUCTURES

Although an industry approach can be helpful in finding potential home-run stocks, you have to go further because the best emerging growth companies are usually too unique to be pigeon-holed into any kind of meaningful industry classification. One important characteristic to look for is a cost structure that can produce favorable operating leverage. This is often found in companies that have relatively high fixed costs. When their sales increase by a given percentage, their total costs go up by a lesser percentage, and this allows their margins to expand. In the short-run, practically any kind of company can experience this kind of leverage. But some emerging growth companies have cost structures that create the possibility of more sustainable profit margin expansion.

One such company is Satellite Music Network. Although its potential is yet to be realized, Satellite Music has the kind of cost structure that may eventually permit significant margin expansion. As its name implies, the company transmits several different formats of radio programming, via satellite, to a network of hundreds of affiliated stations. These affiliates, most of which are located in small markets, then broadcast the programming locally. The major advantage of this system is that it allows the affiliates to broadcast much higher quality programming than they could produce locally, while at the same time it saves them the cost of disk jockey salaries.

What is important is that the programs don't have a canned sound, so the audience thinks it's listening to a locally originated broadcast. This impression is reinforced by playing localized tapes throughout the day. A typical tape mentions a particular community event and includes a specific reference to the local area. Something like "Don't forget to come on down to the bake sale at the Second Presbyterian Church this Saturday." These 5-second tapes are prerecorded by Satellite's disk jockeys and are then automatically inserted in the live broadcasts throughout the day.

The benefits of Satellite Music's pioneering approach to local radio programming have persuaded many of its affiliate stations to become strong advocates. Here are some comments that two of them made in a *New York Times* (3/8/87) article:

> "In the last year, I saved $350,000 on announcers and $500,000 on promotions and give-aways," said Mark Wadlinger, chairman of the Wadlinger Broadcasting Corporation, which owns KZZZ-FM, a station in Kansas City, Kan., that signed up with the Satellite Music Network, a Dallas-based company. "Their announcers are better than what I could hire in Kansas City. Plus, I don't have to put up with the ego of announcers."
>
> "There are a large percentage of our listeners who don't know that the disk jockey's aren't here," said David Williamson, president and general manager of WRSW-FM, an affiliate of the Satellite Music Network in Shelby, Ohio. "Sometimes, they'll come in and say, 'Gee, is there a chance I could talk with the disk jockey,' and we say, 'Yeah, but you have to catch the next plane to Dallas.'"

The affiliates compensate Satellite Music for the programming in two ways. First, they make monthly cash payments. Second, they give up 2 minutes per hour of advertising time, which Satellite then resells to national advertisers. Obviously, the direct cash payments grow as more affiliates are added to the network. But even more important, new affiliates also increase the size of the audience, enabling Satellite to charge higher prices for the advertising time.

Every year since it started, Satellite has added more than 100 affiliates to its network. One way that it has been able to expand at such a fast rate is by adding new formats—country music, then oldies, then big band, then heavy metal, and so on. However, this is an expensive way to grow because it requires more disk jockeys plus more production and satellite transmission expense. As a result, Satellite's costs have so far grown about as fast as its revenue, and it has yet to show a very healthy profit margin.

But there are two leverage points that ought to serve as the foundation for a much higher margin down the road. The first of these should come into play as soon as the company slows down the rate at which it is adding new formats. That will allow higher margins because the cost of producing and distributing the programming is essentially fixed for each of the formats. Whether 10 stations or 200 take the country music programming, the cost of producing and transmitting it is the same. But revenue goes up with every affiliate that is added.

A second leverage point relates to a component of Satellite's cost structure that is called network compensation. This exists because Satellite's audience isn't yet quite large enough to appeal to all national advertisers. To get around this problem, the company buys time from a few major market stations. It then combines this purchased time with the time it receives from its affiliates to achieve the critical mass needed to attract more large advertisers. But as Satellite continues to add affiliates to its network, the audience will eventually reach critical mass on its own. When this happens, purchased time—identified as network compensation in the company's income statement—will become less and less important, until eventually it's not needed at all. So in a few years this cost element will not only flatten out, it could actually disappear altogether. If this happens, it will add over 20 percentage points to pretax margins.

At this writing, Satellite has yet to prove it can earn the healthy profit margins of which it may be capable. Neither has it proven itself to be a home-run stock, and it may never. However, it provides a particularly dramatic illustration of the kind of cost structure that can lead to an unusually large profit margin increase.

PAYCHEX

Opportunities to make sustainable margin improvements are usually less dramatic and less obvious than in the case of Satellite Music. This is particularly true of service businesses, which tend to be people-intensive. To accommodate a higher level of business, service companies must often make a proportionate increase in their number of employees. Therefore, their costs tend to grow in line with revenue, not leaving much room for higher margins. One way around this problem is to increase employee productivity. Paychex, Inc. is an example of a company that was able to do this by improving its data-processing capability. Using upgraded equipment, Paychex's employees were able to do their jobs better, and the productivity increase led to higher margins.

Paychex's business is providing payroll services—preparation of paychecks as well as related reports and tax filings. Rather than attempting to sell its service to all companies large and small, Paychex has chosen to concentrate on the small business segment of the market. It delivers its services to thousands of customers through more than 60 decentralized branch offices that are located throughout the country.

One factor that has helped make this a good business for growth is the enormous size of the potential market. Small businesses in the U.S. number nearly 16 million, and this total is expanding at a healthy rate. Moreover, most of them still do payroll preparation manually. But continuing increases in the complexity of payroll tax regulations will probably force more and more to turn to an outside service for help.

Here is what some of Paychex customers have to say about the advantages of letting it take care of their payroll record-keeping problems:

"Paychex took a big weight off my back," one restaurant owner commented. "Now I can spend more time on things that really impact the bottom line."

"For what they saved us in fines and penalties alone," said the president of an advertising agency, "Paychex paid for themselves several times over."

"There's no way we can prepare payroll internally for what Paychex charges—even though we have a minicomputer," said the president of a franchise chain.

Of course Paychex's market is not uncontested. The best known competitor by far, and probably the toughest, is Automatic Data Processing. ADP has put most of its effort in the big company end of the market, where it is strongest. Paychex's strategy of concentrating on the small business segment, where ADP's reputation has less influence on prospective clients, has so far kept head-to-head competition the exception rather than the rule.

All in all, Paychex has many of the attributes of a classic emerging growth company. It's in a service business that allows it to compete on more than just the basis of price. Its business is stable because the sales cycle is short and there is no inventory cycle to contend with. And because the nature of the service is ongoing, the revenue it generates is recurring. The potential market is very large; and although there is competition, it's

Figure 8.1. Paychex Inc. stock chart. Courtesy of Bridge Information Systems, Inc.

certainly not cutthroat. Nor is it a capital intensive business. All of these qualities have no doubt played an important role in helping Paychex compile the excellent record shown in Table 8.1. But what really made this a home-run stock during 1986 and 1987 was the margin expansion that leveraged up its earnings growth rate.

In 1983 and 1984 Paychex's operating margins averaged a little over 12%, and capital expenditures were quite low. Then in 1985 the company undertook a major program to upgrade its branch office data-processing systems. From less than $3 million in 1984, capital expenditures jumped to nearly $10 million the following year. Initially this program put downward pressure on margins because it caused depreciation charges to increase as a percentage of revenue. But by 1986 the full benefit of the new system began to have a favorable impact on profitability.

Under the old method of operating, the company's payroll specialists received necessary information from their clients over the phone and later filled out forms that had to be keypunched to input the data. The new system brought the operation on-line, allowing the specialists to input the data while they were actually speaking to the client. This change brought about an immediate productivity increase by eliminating the keypunch step.

In addition, however, the new system also had some less obvious benefits. One was a reduction in the amount of input error, which not only made for more satisfied clients but also cut back on the amount of time the payroll specialists had to spend on making corrections. Another benefit of the new system, quite unexpected, was that it made the payroll specialists'

TABLE 8.1 Paychex, Inc. ($000s)

	1984	1985	1986	1987
Revenue	$31,691	$40,930	$50,704	$63,891
Operating Margin	12.8%	11.2%	15.2%	15.7%
Operating Income	4,040	4,594	7,719	10,058
Net Income	2,776	2,982	4,170	5,124
Earnings per Share	$.29	$.35	$.49	$.60
Percentage Change				
Sales	34.1%	29.2%	23.9%	26.0%
Earnings per Share	61.1%	20.7%	40.0%	22.4%
Capital Expenditures	$2,867	$9,978	$3,921	$5,430

SOURCE: Paychex, Inc. annual reports.

job considerably more pleasant. As a result, employee turnover declined, and training expense was reduced significantly.

All together, these productivity improvements more than offset the higher depreciation charges and allowed the operating margin to rise from 11.2% in 1985 to 15.7% in 1987. Although the full impact of this expansion was partially offset by a higher effective tax rate, earnings growth still accelerated to a 40% rate in 1986. Because of multiple expansion, the stock's return was even higher. During most of 1985 it traded in a range of 5 to 8; it hit a high of over 20 during 1987. In just 2 years, Paychex provided investors a fourfold increase, qualifying it as a true home-run stock.

WHAT MADE IT A WINNER

Paychex was an attractive investment for two reasons. First, its fundamental characteristics, particularly its recurring revenue stream, significantly reduced the chance of earnings disappointments. As Tom Golisano, the company's founder and chairman once remarked, "This business is not that hard to run. If we screw it up, we have no one to blame but ourselves." By itself this was good reason to own the stock. But in addition, the company's margin expansion had a leveraged impact on earnings growth and helped the stock attain a higher P/E ratio. This is what took it from being just a good investment to being a home-run stock.

As you consider various candidates for your portfolio, stay alert for companies that have this kind of potential for leveraged earnings growth. They can do wonders for your performance. In the next chapter we'll take a look at a tool that can sometimes help you identify them.

9

Creating and Using Models for Stock Selection

Whether you're trying to discover the next home-run stock ahead of everybody else or dodge a disaster that's about to unfold, it's essential to know all you can about the dynamics of a company's growth. The better you understand what makes a company tick, the more of an edge you'll have relative to other investors. One of the best ways to develop this kind of understanding is by constructing a model—a systematic, quantitative framework for analyzing and forecasting a company's sales and profits. A model is one of the most valuable tools an emerging growth investor can have. By facilitating your understanding of a company's growth dynamics, a model can help you to make more confident projections of future growth. And sometimes it will allow you to spot changing profit trends early, so that you have time to act before they become obvious and are fully reflected in the market.

Although the majority of companies don't lend themselves to accurate modeling, many high-recurring revenue companies are ideal for it. Spectradyne, for instance, is particularly well suited for modeling. Its pay-per-view movie revenue—the heart of its business—can be analyzed with the following equation:

$$\text{Revenue} = \text{Rooms} \times \text{Occupancy Rate} \times \text{Viewing Level} \times \text{Days} \times \text{Price}$$

The five variables on the right-hand side of the equation explain 100% of the company's pay-per-view revenue. A change in any one of them will produce a change in revenue.

This equation can be used as a model for either analyzing past results or forecasting future revenue. For instance, if you know the values for the five variables on the right-hand side of the equation, you can project revenue with complete accuracy. Three of them—rooms, days, and price—are easy to know ahead of time. So it's really necessary to predict only the occupancy rate and the viewing level. And because both of these fluctuate within fairly narrow ranges, it's not difficult to make reasonably accurate revenue forecasts, either on a quarterly or annual basis.

Besides providing a framework that will help you make a more accurate revenue forecast, this kind of model can also be an important tool for understanding and evaluating the variance between forecasts and actual results. Sometimes this will give you an early warning of new trends. For instance, let's say that, in the most recent quarter, Spectradyne's revenue came in 5% below your projection. If the variance was caused by lower occupancy than you had expected, you shouldn't be too concerned. The company has no control over this factor, and it may just represent a random fluctuation caused by weather or some other factor. Or it may be the result of weakness in the economy. In either event, it's reasonable to assume that occupancy will eventually return to normal.

On the other hand, a decline in viewing levels is likely to reflect a more serious problem. Perhaps the proliferation of VCRs and the earlier release of feature movies on cassettes is having a negative effect on viewing. Maybe a weakness has developed in the company's programming capability, and it's not doing as good a job of lining up movies that will appeal to hotel guests. Or maybe there just weren't many good movies available this quarter. Or possibly an unusual event like the Olympics drew viewers away from Spectravision. The model won't provide the answer, but it will help you to ask yourself the right questions and focus your attention on the critical variable.

MEDICINE SHOPPE INTERNATIONAL

To better understand how to go about building and using a model, let's analyze Medicine Shoppe International, a fast-growing company with over 700 franchised pharmacies in operation. If you've ever walked into a pharmacy to have a prescription filled and found that you had to fight your way through aisles of automotive supplies, cosmetics, beer and wine, and beach chairs before you could find the pharmacist, you can be sure that you weren't in a Medicine Shoppe. Unlike the chain drugstores and independents it competes with, a typical Medicine Shoppe pharmacy derives over 90% of its revenue from just filling prescriptions. The stores are small and open only 45 hours per week on average, but they still manage to book prescription sales that on a square foot basis are more than double the industry average.

All of Medicine Shoppe's franchisees are registered pharmacists, most of whom actually operate their own stores. Because these owner–operators aren't distracted by other product lines, they can offer plenty of service and advice to their customers and also fill their prescriptions quickly—all at a very competitive price. Hundreds of pharmacists have found owning one of these franchises an attractive investment because it allows them to increase their income, build equity in a business, and gain more control over their hours and work environment.

The franchisees pay Medicine Shoppe an origination fee when they open their store, plus an ongoing monthly franchise fee for the continuing business and marketing support they receive. These franchise fees constitute a very predictable stream of recurring revenue, which has helped Medicine Shoppe to report higher earnings every quarter since its initial public offering in 1983.

After a few years of really spectacular gains in the early 1980s, operating profit has grown at a 25% to 30% rate since 1984. And it seems likely that this kind of growth can be extended well into the future. With more than 700 units open, it's a good bet that Medicine Shoppe has developed a pattern that works. This is really the key to success in franchising. McDonald's, the greatest franchisor of all times, could never have spread its golden arches throughout the Western world unless it had first developed a pattern for duplicating one profitable restaurant after another in cookie-cutter fashion. Once a company like Medicine Shoppe has developed such a pattern, it still has to recruit competent franchisees, help them get set up in good locations, and then provide the marketing and operational support that will allow them to earn a competitive return on their investment. So high growth isn't totally automatic, but it's certainly attainable and a lot easier to manage than in most other businesses.

THE MODEL

The first step in building an earnings model for Medicine Shoppe is to review the financial statements and other operating data included in its annual report in order to pinpoint where its profits come from. Medicine Shoppe's income statement is shown in the left-hand column of Table 9.1. You can see that the statement breaks revenue into four components,

TABLE 9.1 Medicine Shoppe Income Statement ($000s omitted)

Revenues			
Sales to Franchisees	$4,745	Sales to Franchisees	$4,74■
Franchise Fees	12,610	Cost of Sales to Franchisees	4,16■
Origination Fees	1,172	Gross Profit from Sales	58■
Other	1,298		
Total	19,825	*Other Revenue*	
		Franchise Fees	12,61■
Costs and Expenses		Origination Fees	1,17■
Cost of Sales to Franchisees	4,160	Other	1,29■
Selling, General and Administrative	8,730	Total	15,66■
Total	12,890	Selling, General and Administrative	8,73■
Earnings from Operations	6,935		6,93■
Net Interest Income	524		52■
Earnings before Tax	7,459		7,45■
Tax	3,052		3,05■
Net Income	$4,407		$4,40■
E.P.S.	$.83		$.8■

which total $19,825,000, and it breaks its costs down into just two components, totaling $12,890,000. We'll build a model by considering each of these components separately, and where possible relating them to other variables, as we did with Spectradyne.

Reading down the income statement, the first revenue item is "sales to franchisees," which accounts for 24% of the total. This represents store fixtures, signs, and a small amount of merchandise that Medicine Shoppe sells to the franchisees. Further down the income statement, we see that the first of the two cost elements is "cost of sales to franchisees." Netting this out against sales to franchisees leaves a gross profit of $585,000. If there were no selling, general, and administrative expenses, (s,g,&a) allocated to this activity, it would account for only 8% of the total earnings from operations. But realistically, it must require some s,g,&a, so its contribution is even less than 8%—small enough that we don't have to give it much thought. In fact, because it is so much less important than revenue from the other three sources, it's helpful to just show its gross profit contribution. Recasting the income statement this way (as shown in the right-hand column of Table 9.1) makes it easier to keep your attention focused on the critical variables.

Moving on down the income statement the next item is franchise fees, which at roughly $12.6 million are obviously the most important component of the company's earnings. The management discussion and analysis section of the annual report informs us that these are "based on a percentage of the franchisees' retail sales," which were $315.8 million. The annual report also states that there were 641 pharmacies open at the beginning of the year, and 698 at the end, for an average of 670. From this it's easy to calculate that the average store had revenue of $471,000. With this information, we can set up a simple equation for the company's franchise fee revenue:

Franchise Fees = Fee Percentage × Average Stores × Revenue per Store

or

$12.610 million = 3.99% × 670 × $.471 million

This equation incorporates all three of the variables that determine franchise fee revenue.

Now let's look at Table 9.2, which shows the trends in these three variables. Over the last 5 years all of them have increased quite consistently. Since 1983 the average number of pharmacies in operation has risen from 379 to 670, and the sales per average pharmacy have grown from $355,000 to $471,000. As a result, system sales have increased from $134.5 million to $315.8 million. And Medicine Shoppe's franchise fee revenue has increased at a slightly higher rate since the average franchise fee rate has gone from 3.77% to 3.99% of system sales.

Of these three variables, the one that has grown the fastest and is the most important is the average number of pharmacies in operation. Although construction delays retarded openings in 1987, the number of pharmacies has increased by more than 15% in most years. Moreover, the annual report shows that at the beginning of 1988 there was a backlog of

TABLE 9.2 Variables Affecting Medicine Shoppe Franchise Fees (000s omitted)

	1983	1984	1985	1986	1987
Average Pharmacies	379	444	521	603	670
Sales per Average Pharmacy	$355	$384	$411	$434	$471
System Sales	$134,500	$170,300	$214,000	$261,500	$315,800
Franchise Fee Percentage of System Sales	3.77%	3.93%	3.88%	3.92%	3.99%
Franchise Fee	$5,074	$6,693	$8,296	$10,257	$12,610
Backlog of Unopened Pharmacies	85	117	169	169	179

179 signed franchise agreements for pharmacies that had not yet opened. This backlog is big enough to assure that even if the company can't sell one single franchise more, the existing base will grow by 26%. So we can be quite certain that the trend in this variable will continue to be positive.

We can also be confident that the franchise fee rate will continue to rise as a percentage of system sales. The company's prospectus tells us that for the last few years new franchisees have been paying a fee set at 5.0% of their revenue after the first year of operation. So each new franchise added to the system will help pull up the average rate.

The third variable, sales per average store, is a little more difficult to predict with the same level of certainty. But historically this number has shown consistent increases. And favorable demographics, in the form of an aging population, are at least one reason to expect this trend to persist. So we can be quite confident that at least two, and probably three, of the variables that determine franchise fee revenue will continue to trend upward. This knowledge is quite helpful in permitting a more precise forecast of future revenue from this source.

Continuing down the income statement (Table 9.1), the next revenue item is "origination fees," which are paid to Medicine Shoppe each time a new franchise is opened. Revenue from this source is obviously dependent on the number of new store openings. In a year like 1987, when openings actually declined from the previous year, origination fees also declined.

The fourth and final revenue item is the ever-popular "other." Although the annual report isn't very specific about what goes into this catchall category, it's not hard to figure out that most of it's related to interest on "finance notes receivable." These notes are for loans Medicine Shoppe has made to some of its franchisees to finance their opening costs. The aggregate amount of this interest income will increase as the number of franchises grows but will also fluctuate somewhat with interest rates.

We've actually constructed a model by breaking Medicine Shoppe's revenue down into its components and then relating the major component to three variables. This is a worthwhile exercise because the parts of the model are easier to analyze and project than the whole. So we can make forecasts with greater accuracy and confidence.

The model is also a valuable tool for analyzing actual results. For instance, if the company reports a flat quarter and the stock comes under selling pressure, the model can help you decide what action to take. If the earnings shortfall was due to a random event, it may represent a buying opportunity. On the other hand, if it marks the beginning of a long erosion in profitability (which is often the case when an emerging growth company has a disappointing quarter), it's anything but a buying opportunity,

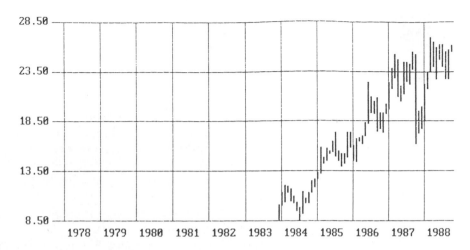

Figure 9.1. Medicine Shoppe International, Inc. stock chart. Courtesy of Bridge Information Systems, Inc.

and you ought to be thinking in terms of bailing out of the stock before it goes even lower. The model can help you decide which of these two scenarios is correct.

Let's say that bad weather resulted in construction delays that have caused the number of new store openings to drop below normal. In this case, origination fees would fall, and there would be no offsetting decline in s,g&a expense, so there would be downward pressure on earnings. If this was the reason for the flat quarter, you're probably safe in assuming it was a one-time event, especially because the company has a long backlog of unopened pharmacies. Earnings will probably get back on track next quarter, and this may well represent an excellent buying opportunity.

However, if the shortfall was caused by a decline in the average revenue per pharmacy, there's a lot more reason to be concerned. Because the store base is so large and geographically widespread, this isn't likely to be a random event—the result of bad weather, for instance. Rather, it's more likely to be the first sign of an adverse trend. Perhaps the industry has become more price competitive, and Medicine Shoppe's market share is beginning to erode. This kind of problem always takes a long time to correct, so the stock weakness is anything but a buying opportunity. In this case your best move will be to sell the stock before it goes down any more, lick your wounds, and move on to a better opportunity.

Simply reading the income statement as it's presented in a quarterly or annual report won't help you decide which of these two scenarios is correct. To do that you have to go a step further: Take the data and analyze it with a model like the one we've developed.

ENTERTAINMENT PUBLICATIONS

The most valuable kind of model is one that projects trends in profit margins as well as sales. As we discussed in the last chapter, home-run stocks usually owe their great performance to favorable earnings surprises caused by profit margin expansion. Conversely, earnings shortfalls are often the result of contracting margins. Therefore, a systematic way of anticipating changes in a company's profit margins can be enormously useful.

Entertainment Publications is an example of a company that lends itself particularly well to modeling both revenue and profit margins. Its major product line is a series of discount coupon books, called Entertainment Books. These books, which the company publishes in more than 80 different geographic markets, contain hundreds of coupons offering special discounts on area restaurants, hotels, theaters, concerts, sporting events, and other leisure activities.

Restaurants account for the majority of the coupons. A typical coupon offers a second dinner entree free when one is purchased at the regular menu price. This is a good, low-cost way for a restaurant to build up its clientele by attracting new customers. In contrast to media advertising, this form of marketing entails no risk because the coupons cost the restaurant nothing if they fail to bring in new business. All kinds of establishments, from fast-food stands to upscale gourmet places, have used Entertainment coupons to draw new customers.

Although restaurants account for over half the coupons in a typical Entertainment Book, hotels, theaters, museums, orchestras, and sports teams also use them as a marketing tool. In addition to attracting new customers, the coupons generate incremental revenue by filling up space that would otherwise be unoccupied.

Entertainment Publications sells most of its books on consignment through various nonprofit organizations, like the Boy Scouts and the Lions Club, who use them for fund raising. The buyer usually feels that he is supporting a worthy cause, and because he only needs to use two or three coupons to come out ahead, it's not hard to make a sale. The books are typically priced at $25 or $30, of which the selling organization keeps about 20% as a commission.

The business is highly seasonal; most of the books are sold in the fall or winter, and the coupons expire at the end of the following summer. The lead time for a new market to become profitable is quite long because the company must start work 6 months or more in advance of the scheduled publication date. The organizations that will sell the books and the local businesses that will offer the coupons all have to be lined up. And, of course, the book itself must be printed. All of this cost is incurred and expensed before any revenue is generated. As a result of these heavy front-end costs, a new edition invariably loses money in its first year and usually doesn't turn profitable until its second or third year of publication. But after the breakeven point is passed, margins expand rapidly. And by the time a market reaches maturity, it should be very profitable.

THE MODEL

Entertainment Publications' income statements are shown in Table 9.3. In analyzing them, it's essential to keep in mind that new markets lose money, whereas mature markets earn high margins. This basic principle, which is obvious from reading the company's annual reports, is so fundamentally important that it can be used as the foundation for building a model of the Entertainment Book business.

Information from annual reports and 10-k's can be used to construct a schedule of the company's various markets according to their age. For in-

TABLE 9.3 Entertainment Publications, Inc. ($000s omitted)

Year Ending 6/30	1983	1984	1985	1986	1987
Revenue					
Entertainment Books	$16,600	$20,500	$23,900	$30,600	$37,500
Other	3,696	5,871	9,042	10,263	16,128
Total	20,296	26,371	32,942	40,863	53,628
Operating Profit Margin	21.5%	21.8%	10.6%	15.2%	16.5%
Operating Profit	4,356	5,733	3,450	6,200	8,834
Other Income, Net	384	950	1,706	1,641	1,544
Pretax Income	4,740	6,683	5,196	7,841	10,378
Tax	2,181	3,006	2,162	3,314	4,475
Minority Interest	153	(59)	(422)	(21)	31
Net Income from					
Continuing Operations	$ 2,406	$ 3,736	$ 3,456	$ 4,548	$ 5,872
E.P.S. from Continuing					
Operations	$.67	$.98	$.87	$1.07	$1.23

stance, the 84 markets in which the company was active during 1987 had the following distribution in terms of maturity:

Age	Number
Startup	12
1 Year	7
2 Years	17
3 Years	12
4 Years or More	36
Total	84

It's also possible to draw up similar schedules for earlier years. With these you can construct a model like the one shown here to approximate the way an average market evolves from startup to maturity. This model was developed by finding, through trial-and-error repetition, the set of numbers that provided the closest fit to the actual revenue and profit margin data:

	Startup	Year 1	Year 2	Year 3	Year 4
Revenue (000s)	0	$ 200	$ 400	$ 600	$ 650
Operating margin	Negative	Negative	0.0%	33.3%	38.5%
Operating profit/(loss)	(200)	(150)	0	200	250

When these revenue and profit margin assumptions are multiplied by the number of markets in each stage of development and the totals are added up, you get a good approximation of the actual numbers:

	BOOK SALES		OPERATING PROFIT MARGIN	
6/30 Fiscal Year	Model	Actual	Model	Actual
1982	$12.5	$12.6	18.0%	18.8%
1983	16.5	16.6	20.6	21.5
1984	19.5	20.5	15.1	21.7
1985	24.2	23.9	9.3	10.6
1986	31.3	30.6	15.3	15.2
1987	38.8	37.5	20.5	16.5

The model does best at forecasting sales. Its average error is within a ± 2% range, and even the largest variance is less than 5%. The projections of operating margins are good, too, but for several reasons they're not quite as accurate as the revenue numbers. For one thing, the Entertainment Books account for only about 70% of the company's business. The model doesn't take into account the other product lines, which also affect the actual operating profit margins. In fact, low margins or actual losses in some of these other businesses were probably a significant reason why the actual operating margin was below the projected level in 1987.

Another limitation is the model's inability to take into account all of the factors that directly influence the books' margins. For instance, price increases and changes in the cost of paper aren't considered. However, it appears that market development, the sole factor on which the model is based, is clearly the most important single variable in explaining the company's profitability.

A major strong point of the model is the good job it does of predicting the direction that changes in the operating margin will take. For instance, it correctly forecast the margin uptick that occurred in 1983. In 1984 it called for a downturn because of the large number of startup markets. The pressure didn't actually show up until the following year, but then margins declined sharply to the approximate level called for by the model. By 1986 the newer markets were approaching profitability, and the pace of startups had slowed. On this basis, the model correctly predicted the start of a new uptrend in margins.

The model can actually be used as a decision-making tool because it fulfills two essential requirements. First, it makes sense as a logical way of

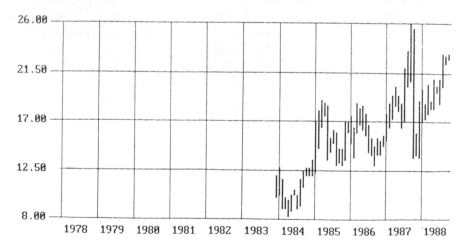

Figure 9.2. Entertainment Publications, Inc. stock chart. Courtesy of Bridge Information Systems, Inc.

explaining changes in the company's revenue and profitability. Its underlying principle is that mature markets contribute healthy profits, whereas startups lose money. You need only read the company's annual reports to see that this is valid. Second, the model's projections fit the actual data quite closely. This allows you to be confident that it captures enough of the company's true dynamics to be legitimate as a forecasting tool. If the projections didn't fit the actual data reasonably well, you would have to conclude that factors other than market development were more important. Conversely, if the projections were accurate, but the model didn't make intuitive sense, you would be reluctant to use it for fear the fit was more the result of luck than cause and effect.

BUILDING A MODEL

The way to develop a model like the ones we've discussed is to start with the variables you think have the most influence on a company's sales and profits. Most of these should be pretty obvious from reading annual reports, 10-k's, articles, and research material. At the same time, list whatever relevant numbers you can find in the same sources. Massage this data every way that makes sense to see if you can fit it to the variables you have in mind.

A personal computer with a spreadsheet program will help a lot with the number crunching, but all you really need is a calculator. The most important ingredients, however, are imagination and an enjoyment of playing with numbers. It's basically a trial-and-error process. If you can't get a good fit with the first variable, try another one. Just keep fiddling with the numbers until they fall into place.

Developing a model obviously demands a lot of time and effort, and some companies simply don't lend themselves to it. But the effort will invariably help you develop a better understanding of the company's growth dynamics. And if you're successful in constructing an accurate model, you may gain an important edge in terms of anticipating future changes in profitability. It might even help you spot the next home-run stock—before it's on its way out of the park.

10

Valuing Individual
Stocks

By now you should have a good understanding of the business characteristics that give certain companies an edge in being able to deliver high
growth without stumbling and the characteristics that make others more
susceptible to earnings shortfalls and disappointing stock performance.
This understanding is critical to good stock selection, which is the backbone of the portfolio management process. But there is still one more step
that's an essential part of constructing a portfolio. You also have to consider
valuation. Up until this point, we've been talking more about companies,
as opposed to stocks. It's necessary to distinguish between the two, for
even if your portfolio is full of fine little companies that consistently come
through with strong earnings growth, your performance won't be very
good unless you buy the stocks at reasonable prices.

Let's say that based on the New Horizons' relative P/E, the emerging
growth universe looks attractively valued. You want to get started, and
you've identified 20 or so stocks that you think are attractive candidates
for your portfolio. All of them meet the basic selection standards we've
discussed. They all have good records, strong balance sheets, and earn a
high return on equity. They operate in business environments that are conducive to rapid growth, and they have limited competition. Moreover,
most of them have good visibility, so their managements should be able to
keep them under control even though they're growing rapidly. Now you
need just one more thing: a framework for judging how cheap or expen-

119

sive each of the stocks is relative to the others. This is essential because valuations always vary significantly within the emerging growth universe.

Most professional investors use a dividend discount model to calculate the "intrinsic value" of a stock. They project future cash flows—both dividends and a price at which the stock will eventually be sold—and then discount them back to the present at a rate that includes an appropriate premium for risk. This method, which is sensitive to changes in interest rates as well as earnings and dividend projections, has long been accepted as a theoretically correct approach to valuation. In practice it works quite well for relatively stable stocks that pay high dividends, and it's also easily applied to bonds. However, it's a lot harder to use with emerging growth stocks because they almost never pay a meaningful dividend, and essentially all of their value is in the price you assume for the end of the holding period. Analysts and investors often deal with this problem by estimating an underlying earnings growth rate and then calculating the ratio of the stock's P/E multiple to this growth rate. For instance, if a company is expected to grow at a 25% rate and its stock sells at $20 \times$ earnings, its P/E is 80% of its growth rate:

$$\frac{\text{P/E Ratio} = 20 \times}{\text{Growth Rate} = 25\%} = 80\%$$

This is a handy way of comparing stocks with different growth rates and P/E ratios. It's very common to see research reports that take this approach to valuation. An analyst will support his recommendation with a statement something like this: "Selling at only $17 \times$ earnings, a P/E ratio that is less than half the 35% growth rate we are projecting, the stock appears to be undervalued. We strongly recommend purchase."

You should recognize this method for what it is: at best nothing more than a very quick and dirty first pass at valuation. To endow it with any more meaning than this is a serious mistake. Yet most investors go no further in thinking about valuation.

LOOKING AT THE WRONG HALF OF THE EQUATION

The problem with the P/E-to-growth approach to valuation is that it conveniently implies all of the risk is related to possible contraction in the stock's P/E ratio. It completely ignores the chance that earnings will fail to grow as expected. Unfortunately, this is a reversal of the way things actually work. It's quite rare for an emerging growth stock to meet earnings expectations year after year and still be a disappointing performer because of multiple contraction. You're much more likely to lose money with a stock that fails to deliver the earnings growth expected of it.

To understand how this emphasis on P/E risk can be misleading, let's consider two emerging growth companies, both of which are expected to earn $1.00 per share this year and grow at a 25% rate thereafter. Assuming they actually grow as expected, each company will earn $3.05 in 5 years. Company A's stock sells at 16× earnings, whereas Company B's stock has a multiple of 20×. For the same earnings and the same growth rate, an investor has to pay a 25% higher multiple for Company B. This seems like a big premium. But if Company B's earnings actually do grow at the expected 25% rate, long-term investors will earn a positive return unless the P/E ratio suffers enormous contraction.

	COMPANY A			COMPANY B		
	EPS	P/E	Stock Price	EPS	P/E	Stock Price
PRICE						
Today	$1.00 ×	16.00	= 16	$1.00 ×	20.00	= 20
5 Years	$3.05 ×	5.25	= 16	$3.05 ×	6.55	= 20

As shown here, Company B's P/E ratio would have to decline below 6.55× for an investor to incur a loss. It's hard to imagine a multiple this low ever being applied to a company growing this fast. Of course, Company A could withstand even greater multiple contraction before a loss would be incurred. But so what? Both of these are such low valuations you can practically forget about them as being realistic possibilities.

In this example, Company B may have slightly greater multiple risk, but the real risk in both stocks is not in the multiple at all. Rather, it's in the possibility that earnings won't come through as projected. If Company A is still earning $1.00 5 years from now, its 16× P/E ratio will be high in retrospect. And if it doesn't have any earnings at all, you will in fact have paid an infinite multiple for it. On the other hand, if Company B actually does grow at 25%, its 20× P/E will seem like a bargain looking back.

HIDDEN RISK

Many investors who use the P/E-to-growth approach to valuation take it to its logical conclusion and structure their portfolio in a way that gives them a target growth rate for the lowest possible P/E ratio. In terms of the example shown previously, they will always substitute Company A for Company B. This seems like a good way to optimize their risk/reward ratio. After all, they ask, why pay 20× earnings if you can get the same growth at $16 \times$? In fact, however, these investors are usually stacking their portfolio with a lot more risk than they realize. By attempting to keep the P/E ratio as low as possible, they end up owning too many second-rate companies that will fail to deliver good earnings growth.

This tendency is reflected in something I've observed frequently: When an emerging growth portfolio is divided in half according to P/E ratio, the high multiple group usually outperforms the low multiple group of stocks. On average, the high P/E group includes just as many winners but fewer losers. Although I have no way of proving it, I suspect this is quite typical.

One thing that has probably helped reinforce the tendency of many investors to overemphasize P/E risk is the popularity enjoyed by the value approach to investing. One of the principles of this style is to limit risk by concentrating heavily on low P/E stocks. There is no doubt that the value approach is a valid style, appropriate for many investors. Historically it has produced good results, and its advocates include many well-known and highly successful investors. But it's very different from emerging growth investing, and trying to combine the two styles hardly ever works. It's possible to eliminate a lot of the P/E risk in a value portfolio but not in an emerging growth portfolio. When you try, you usually end up owning a lot of junk.

Another factor that contributes to the overemphasis of P/E risk is that it's so much easier to measure than fundamental risk. It doesn't take any brilliant analysis, or even any work, to observe that Company B in our earlier example has more P/E risk than Company A. But the higher multiple doesn't necessarily make it a riskier investment overall. To determine that, you also have to take into account the earnings or fundamental risk of the two companies—something that is considerably more complicated than just comparing P/E ratios.

By no means am I suggesting that you should ignore P/E ratios altogether and blithely pay any multiple for a high-quality company, thinking that the earnings will always bail you out in the long run. If you do this, you'll almost certainly end up with a portfolio full of trendy stocks, many of which are faddish and overpriced. But you should also guard against the very common tendency to overemphasize P/E risk. It will always lead you to own a portfolio full of doggy companies that don't grow the way you expect them to and are never as cheap as you thought.

MEASURING FUNDAMENTAL RISK

Fundamental risk may be more important than P/E risk, but it is also much, much harder to get a handle on. It's influenced by a lot of factors, some of which don't lend themselves to quantitative measurement, and all of which are difficult to assign a proper weight. It's easy to argue that one company is of higher quality than another and that its stock should carry a higher P/E ratio because of the higher assurance the earnings will actually be realized. But it is much more difficult to say just how big that premium should be.

Although fundamental risk is hard to quantify, I think the effort is more than worthwhile. To cope with the problem, I've found it useful to grade stocks with a system that takes into account 10 valuation factors:

Factor	Points
1. Visibility/Recurring Revenue	16
2. Maturity	12
3. Competitive	12
4. Distribution	10
5. Momentum	10
6. Return on Equity	7
7. Balance Sheet Strength	7
8. Cash Flow	6
9. Growth Rate	10
10. Accounting	10
TOTAL	100

As you can see, all 10 categories combined are worth a maximum score of 100. However, not every category is weighted equally. The most important is Visibility/Recurring Revenue with a maximum score of 16; from there the number of possible points declines.

Now let's see how the system works in practice. In the following description, we'll use Paychex as an example:

1. *Visibility/Recurring Revenue* (16 points). I believe this is the single most important characteristic an emerging growth company can have. As we have seen, rapid growth creates enormous strain. Good visibility gives a company a big advantage in coping with this strain. It allows management to anticipate problems before they become serious, making it much easier to maintain control and reducing the risk of earnings shortfalls. Best of all is a recurring revenue base. It's much easier to start every year from a base close to the prior year's level of sales than it is to start from scratch.

To score the maximum 16 points in this category, over 90% of a company's revenue should be recurring. Paychex comes very close to the maximum, but I have docked it 1 point because each year it must replace over 10% of its starting contracts. This turnover reflects the high mortality rate among Paychex's small business customers, rather than a dissatisfaction with its service.

Companies at the low end of the visibility scale are typically manufacturers of big-ticket items with cyclical demand. For instance, I would give Zycad no more than a single point in this category.

2. *Maturity* (12 points). Very few emerging growth companies ever develop or acquire a second product line that is as successful as their first. In the case of Hogan Systems, we saw a particularly dramatic example of how risky it can be to invest in a company whose continued growth is heavily dependent on the successful introduction of a new product. A company whose key product line is maturing or has already saturated a significant portion of the available market always carries above-average risk. This is especially true in a crowded market or in a business where it's possible for a competitor to get a jump on new technology.

I have given Paychex a relatively high 10 out of 12 possible points in this category. The 70,000 clients it had at the end of its 1987 fiscal year represented only a small percentage of the nearly 16 million small businesses in the country. Although many of these will probably never use automated payroll services, the market is still a long way from being saturated. A slight negative, however, is that with over 70 sales and service locations already open, Paychex's potential growth from geographic expansion is limited.

3. *Competition* (12 points). The best emerging growth companies have some proprietary advantage that shields them from excessive competition in their particular market niche. This allows them to capture most of the growth that's available, while still operating profitably enough to finance most of their expansion with retained earnings. For instance, Computer Associates and Spectradyne are both companies whose growth was facilitated by the dominant positions they were able to establish within their own market niches.

In this category, Paychex scores 9 out of a possible 12 points. It loses 3 points because there is nothing particularly proprietary about its service, and ADP, its major competitor, is a lot bigger and better known. If Paychex were in a manufacturing rather than a service business, its score would be ever lower.

On the plus side, however, the company has a large investment in proprietary software that would be difficult and expensive to duplicate. Also, a new office usually has to be open for several years before it becomes profitable. These factors have been a deterrent on the number of startup competitors attempting to enter local markets.

4. *Distribution* (10 points). A company that depends on distributors rather than marketing through its own direct sales force is at least one step removed from its ultimate customer and therefore gives up a measure of

control over its own destiny. Moreover, at some stage of its growth, it will probably want to invest in developing a direct sales force. This is invariably a tricky hurdle, and companies that have not yet cleared it carry an extra degree of risk. Riskier still are companies that sell their product to original equipment manufacturers because they are even one step further removed from their ultimate customer. As we have seen in the case of the semiconductor industry, they have to contend with inventory cycles that cause volatility and make a business difficult to manage.

Paychex scores the maximum possible 10 points in this category because it sells to and deals directly with its ultimate customer. This is typical of service companies, most of which would score high in this category.

5. *Momentum* (10 points). A company whose growth rate is accelerating—whether through margin expansion, greater product acceptance, or a new found competitive edge—is more likely to come through with favorable earnings surprises than one whose growth rate is slowing. This category measures momentum by comparing growth in the most recent quarter to the average growth rate of the four preceding quarters. A down quarter rates 0 and a flat quarter 1. A quarter that is up, but up less than 10%, gets a 2. Up more than 10%, but less than the average growth of the four preceding quarters, rates a 4. A constant growth rate ± 2% gets a 6. Higher scores are given for accelerating growth, with the maximum 10 points going to companies whose most recent quarterly growth rate is at least 10% above the preceding four quarters. Obviously a company's momentum score must be recalculated quarterly.

At this writing, Paychex's most recent quarter was right in line with the average growth for the four preceding quarters, so it rates a 6. Be careful using this system with companies whose earnings have recently been depressed because it will overstate their momentum. In those cases you should make subjective downward adjustments.

6. *Return on Equity* (7 points). This measure, the ratio of a company's net income to the average of its beginning equity and ending equity, is the best indicator of fundamental profitability. It determines how much growth can be financed internally and what kind of dividends the company will eventually be able to pay out to shareholders after it matures. Companies whose return is less than 10% get no points. A return of 28% or higher is required to score the maximum 7 points.

At just over 24%, Paychex scores 6 points out of a possible 7. When you apply this measure, watch out for companies that are overcapitalized. Some high-quality, small companies take a very conservative approach to financing their business and have a disproportionately high percentage of their assets in cash or short-term investments that yield much lower returns than they earn on their operating assets. This depresses the return on equity measure artificially and should be adjusted for.

7. *Balance Sheet Strength* (7 points). Some companies are able to earn a high return on equity because they borrow to finance their operations. The problem with debt financing is that it adds risk; by magnifying fluctuations in a company's operating profitability, it increases earnings volatility. Table 10.1 illustrates how this works. In this example, both companies have the same level of sales and the same operating margin, and both are expected to earn $1.00 per share. The only difference between the two is that Company A has no debt on its balance sheet, whereas Company B has exactly as much debt as equity. As a result, Company B incurs interest expense and therefore has a lower aftertax margin, even though its operating margin is the same as Company A's. If some adverse development causes operating profit to come in at $7 million, instead of the expected $9 million, Company A's earnings will drop to $.78 per share. But because it must pay a fixed amount of interest expense, Company B will experience a larger shortfall; its earnings would drop to $.69.

Besides their greater volatility, companies with a lot of debt are also more dependent on external funding for future growth. Consequently, existing shareholders are more likely to be diluted by future equity offerings.

Although Paychex actually carries a small amount of debt in the form of a low-cost industrial revenue bond that it issued to finance its headquarters building, it has more than enough money in surplus cash and short-term investments to offset this debt. Therefore, I would award it the maximum score of 7 points. At the other extreme, companies whose debt exceeds their equity receive no points.

TABLE 10.1 The Extra Risk Created by Debt Financing ($000,000s omitted)

	COMPANY A		COMPANY B	
Debt	—		20	
Equity	40		20	
Total Capital	40		40	
	Budget	*Actual*	*Budget*	*Actual*
Sales	$60.0	$60.0	$60.0	$60.0
Operating Margin	15.0%	11.7%	15.0%	11.7%
Operating Profit	9.0	7.0	9.0	7.0
Interest Expense	—	—	2.5	2.5
Pretax Profit	9.0	7.0	6.5	4.5
Tax @ 40%	3.6	2.8	2.6	1.8
Net Income	$5.4	$4.2	$3.9	$2.7
Shares Outstanding	5.4	5.4	3.9	3.9
E.P.S.	$1.00	$.78	1.00	$.69

8. *Cash Flow* (6 points). Although investors focus most of their attention on earnings, this one number doesn't tell the whole story; cash flow is also important. Ultimately companies need cash, not earnings, to pay for the capital expenditures and other investments necessary to accommodate future growth. High cash flow also gives a stock underlying support if the company's earnings should turn down. And when the company eventually matures and its growth begins to slow, high cash flow, like a high return on equity, will support a more generous dividend payout.

With a ratio of cash flow to net income just over $1.7\times$, Paychex gets 4 points out of a possible 6 in this category. To receive the maximum score of 6 points, a company's cash flow from operations should be at least $2.0\times$ its net income. Spectradyne would qualify for this maximum score, as would most cable TV operators.

9. *Growth Rate* (10 points). This is the one valuation factor that most investors focus on and seldom go beyond. But here it accounts for just 10 points because the system is designed to be used only with emerging growth companies, and, within this limited universe, growth-rate differences are narrower than they would be across a broader spectrum of stocks.

Also, the faster a small company grows, the more likely it is to get out of control. So a lot of the advantage of higher growth is offset by greater risk. This is another reason for limiting the growth rate score to just 10 points.

I use the following point values for various growth rates:

Growth Rate	Points
Under 20%	2
20%–24%	4
25%–29%	6
30%–34%	8
35%–40%	9
Over 40%	10

With an estimated growth rate of 25%, Paychex scores 6 points out of a possible 10 in this category.

10. *Accounting* (10 points). This category is included to even out the impact of particularly liberal or conservative accounting policies. Like most companies, Paychex rates a neutral score of 5. If it capitalized a lot of its software development costs or for some reason had an unusually low tax rate, its score would be lower. On the other hand, if it expensed a discretionary item that really represented investment in future growth, its score would be adjusted upward.

You may have noticed that one category that's not included in this system is management. No doubt some investors would take sharp exception to this exclusion. However, I've yet to see evidence that anyone can do a consistently good job at evaluating management. Moreover, individual investors don't have the necessary access to even try.

USING THE SYSTEM

Paychex's score, 78 out of a maximum possible 100 points, is recapped in Table 10.2. By itself, this score doesn't have much meaning. To use it for valuation purposes, you have to compare it to the stock's P/E ratio and then see how this relationship holds up against other emerging growth stocks. You can do this with a scatter diagram like the one shown in Figure 10.1. Plot each stock's fundamental score on the horizontal axis and its P/E ratio on the vertical axis. At a minimum, you should do this for at least 15 or 20 different stocks; the more you include, the more accurate your perspective.

Most stocks will score in a range of 40 to 85 points and will be clustered around an imaginary line that slopes up from the bottom-left corner of the chart. The higher a stock's score, the higher the P/E ratio you expect to pay for it. Stocks that are way above the imaginary line look to be overvalued, and stocks that are way below it appear undervalued relative to the alternatives. For instance, let's say that we find four other stocks that have scores within a point or two of Paychex's 78, and they all have P/E ratios of 18× earnings. If Paychex's P/E is 22×, it will be well above the line, reflecting apparent overvaluation. At 14×, it would appear undervalued, and would show up below the line.

This valuation system attempts to quantify all of the factors that influ-

TABLE 10.2 Recap of Paychex's Score

Factor	Maximum Points	Paychex
Visibility/Recurring Revenue	16	15
Maturity	12	10
Competition	12	9
Distribution	10	10
Momentum	10	6
Return on Equity	7	6
Balance Sheet Strength	7	7
Cash Flow	6	4
Growth Rate	10	6
Accounting	10	5
Total	100	78

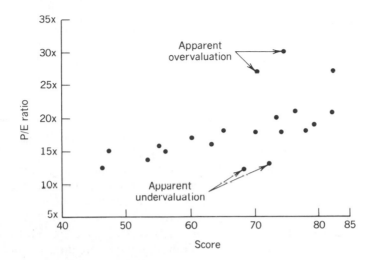

Figure 10.1. P/E ratio versus fundamental score.

ence what multiple a knowledgeable investor should be willing to pay for a given company's earnings. Its purpose is to help you identify stocks that appear to be either overvalued or undervalued relative to their peers. But you should recognize that, like any valuation system, this one will have some imperfections. So use it as a guide, rather than an absolute authority for making investment decisions. Try to figure out why a stock appears to be mispriced. Is it overvalued because of an investment fad that's likely to fade away in a few months, or is it because the system does not take adequate account of some fundamental factor? The market may not always be perfectly efficient at valuing small stocks, but it's also rare that a gross distortion lasts for very long. So if you think that a stock is ridiculously undervalued, be sure to take a second look. Maybe you just didn't realize that IBM is poised to enter the market with a new product that might blow your company away.

QUALITY OF EARNINGS

Some companies have higher quality earnings than others, and this can have a big impact on stock valuation. The system described here makes an effort to take this into account through the 10 points awarded for accounting policy. But earnings quality often goes beyond just how liberal or conservative a company is in recognizing revenue and capitalizing costs. Three factors in particular often have a significant effect on the earnings quality and valuation of emerging growth stocks:

1. Tax loss carryforwards.
2. Interest income.
3. The level of research and development spending.

Tax loss carryforwards are particularly common among small high-tech companies because they often go through several years of product development before they generate any revenue. Practically every biotech company, for instance, fits this profile. During the development period, substantial losses are inevitable because, without a product to sell, there is no revenue to cover research and other expenses. Once these companies become profitable, their past losses can be deducted from current profits for income tax purposes. For a year or two, there may be no tax liability at all, but eventually the loss carryforwards will be used up, and the company will have to accrue for taxes. When this happens, it may report lower per-share earnings, even if pretax income increases 50% or more. So always check a company's tax rate and be sure to figure the stock's P/E ratio on the basis of fully taxed earnings.

Another item to watch out for is disproportionately high interest income. Many emerging growth companies shun the use of debt financing because they don't want to take on the added risk of financial leverage. And if their P/E ratio is high, equity capital is less expensive than debt anyway. Companies that adopt such a conservative financial policy sometimes become overcapitalized, holding much more money in cash equivalents or short-term investments than they need for running the business. The interest income earned on these surplus funds can account for a meaningful percentage of their total earnings. However, it certainly doesn't deserve any kind of multiple because it will eventually disappear if the cash is drawn down to finance capital expenditures or acquisitions. So be careful to use a P/E ratio that is calculated only on the company's earnings from operations.

A third item to stay alert for is the level of research and development expense; some small companies are disproportionately big spenders in this area. Collagen Corp., for instance, is a particularly striking example of a company whose valuation is affected by its heavy r&d effort. This company derives almost all of its revenue from the sale of injectable collagen, a material used by dermatologists and plastic surgeons to treat wrinkles and acne scars. For several years, Collagen's sales have grown at a respectable but unspectacular 15%–20% rate, while its earnings have bounced all around. In spite of this unspectacular record, the stock has often traded at a P/E ratio in excess of 40× earnings.

The reason for this high valuation becomes apparent when you examine the company's income statement and realize that it has been spending more than 30% of its revenue for research and development. The injectable collagen business clearly doesn't require this level of r&d support. If this were the company's only business, it wouldn't have to plow any more than 10% of its revenue back into research to continue growing nicely. The rest of the research spending is supporting the development of proprietary, collagen-based new products that will address potentially large markets, such as cancer treatment and bone healing. Taking this into account, Collagen's base of existing business is a lot more profitable than it appears at first glance, and the stock's P/E is not so high when it is calculated on "normalized" earnings.

PERCEPTIONS

Heavy r&d spending and other factors that affect the quality of a company's earnings aren't the only things that cause valuations that may seem out of line. Just as often, they're the result of extremes in the way investors perceive a company. Condom manufacturers and television shopping networks are but two examples of stock groups that in recent years have risen to unrealistic levels because investors got carried away with their enthusiasm. These extremes in perception are seldom sustainable. Usually it takes no more than a downward revision in earnings estimates to change today's high-quality growth "concept" into tomorrow's investment equivalent of the hoola hoop. This is where a systematic approach to valuation, such as the one we have discussed here, can really be useful. Fad stocks always show up way above the imaginary line because their fundamentals can't support their P/E ratios.

Sometimes, however, changes in perception work in favor of the long-term investor. As we discussed earlier, this was true in the case of Spectradyne. Just prior to becoming a buy-out candidate, this stock traded at a P/E in the low 20s. At best, its valuation looked reasonable; it certainly didn't seem to be on the bargain table. Yet the company was bought out at approximately twice this price. Clearly, the buyers' perception of value was different from the market's. The investor group that took the company over, quite reasonably, believed the proper way to value it was on a multiple of cash flow rather than earnings. Those shareholders who recognized that an eventual acquisition would be made on this basis were well rewarded for holding the stock through occasional periods of apparent overvaluation. In the end, their perception of value proved to be the correct one.

Personal computer software stocks are another group that experienced a positive change in perception. Initially investors worried that this business would be as volatile and competitive as video games, to which it seemed analogous in many respects. But over time it became apparent that very definite standards were developing among users. For instance, Lotus 1-2-3 would be the accepted spreadsheet program, and Ashton-Tate's d-Base the standard for data base management. Other companies might bring out very acceptable alternatives at lower prices, but most users would remain loyal to the standards because they were comfortable with them and already knew how to use them. And in large organizations with data-processing networks, the standards were further strengthened by the need for software compatibility. As these trends came into focus, investors started considering the companies more stable and better shielded from competition, and they became willing to pay higher multiples for the stocks.

Anticipating changes in investor perception is seldom easy. It requires the imagination to discount events over a longer time horizon than the market uses. Even with a lot of experience this is difficult, but it's always worth trying. Ask yourself, "How is the market going to look at this stock 6 months or a year from now? Is it likely to gain greater investor recognition? Will growth rate expectations increase? Will investor confidence in that growth rate change? Is there some other factor that may lead investors to pay a higher multiple for this company's earnings?" Guessing the correct answers to these questions can do a lot to help your performance.

DIVERSIFICATION

Finally, we ought to give some thought to portfolio diversification. There are two main points to keep in mind. First, any emerging growth stock portfolio should spread its risk over a minimum of about 10 different stocks. If you can only find, say, seven attractive candidates that you want to buy at today's prices, you can always get the extra diversification you need by investing the rest of the portfolio in a mutual fund. Second, use some common sense in spreading your bets across different economic sectors and industries. If some adverse development hits an industry across the board, you don't want 40% of your portfolio exposed. So if you're only going to own 10 stocks, make sure that 4 of them aren't software companies or specialty retailers—even if they do show up as being the cheapest stocks in your universe.

Beyond these two points, don't worry too much about diversification. To a large extent, all emerging growth stocks move together as a group no matter what industry they're in. And anyway, emerging growth should never represent more than just a part of your overall investment program. This is really the most important consideration in diversifying your assets.

Part III
Buying and Selling

11

Liquidity and
Trading Strategies

Once you've selected the stocks you want to own in your portfolio and have determined whether or not they are reasonably priced, you still have to execute the trades. Many investors simply call their broker, place the order, and never give any further thought to the trading function. Nine times out of ten there is no reason to. But occasionally the volatility of emerging growth stocks will create special trading opportunities. Whether or not you attempt to take advantage of these opportunities, you should still be aware of the factors that cause them. For the most part, they are the result of the illiquidity that's so typical of this sector of the market.

During April 1987, two different stocks—one large and one small— were negatively affected by unrelated news events that drove them lower. The contrast in their price action offers a vivid illustration of the difference in liquidity between large capitalization stocks and emerging growth stocks. First, Texaco, the giant oil company, was ordered by the Supreme Court to post a $12-billion appeals bond in its continuing legal battle with Pennzoil over the acquisition of Getty Oil. As a result of this ruling, Texaco would file for Chapter XI bankruptcy protection a few days later. The *Wall Street Journal* offered this description of trading: "The ruling touched off frantic trading in Texaco common, which plunged $4, to close at $33.625 a share, on volume of 5.9 million shares, making it the most active issue in New York Stock Exchange composite trading yesterday." The $4 price drop meant the stock lost 10.63% of its value in that day's trading.

At about the same time CompuTrac, a small software company specializing in data-processing systems for law offices, announced that its first quarter earnings would be down. The *Wall Street Journal* (4/14/87, p. 53) provided the following coverage:

> CompuTrac Inc. said it expects per-share net income for its first quarter ending April 30 to decline between 50% and 60% from year-earlier profit because of shipment delays. . . .
>
> The company said that sales commitments are about 50% above last year, but said it will only recognize about 30% to 40% of the commitments that it will ship during the period.
>
> CompuTrac, which makes computer systems designed for the legal profession and information retrieval systems, said the delay in shipments is the result of various factors, including customers being unable to accept delivery until office moves are completed, completion of a pending merger, and delays because of heavy demand from a hardware supplier.
>
> "The company said it does not expect the drop in its first quarter earnings to have an impact on its full year. The company said "we anticipate our earnings strength will be in the second half of the year."

Although the CompuTrac news was certainly disappointing to shareholders, it was the kind of thing that has to be expected occasionally from a small company that sells only a few high-priced systems each quarter. It wasn't CompuTrac's first down quarter, nor was it likely to be its last. Investors could take heart from the fact that orders were actually up about 50% and that the company had not lowered its own expectations for full-year earnings. Clearly, CompuTrac was saying this was a short-term problem attributable to the vagaries of the business, rather than a reflection of any serious fundamental weakness. Yet on the day of this announcement, CompuTrac stock fell slightly more than 20%. On a percentage basis, it declined almost twice as much as Texaco, whose problems seemed just a bit more severe.

Another particularly vivid example of the illiquidity of small capitalization stocks occurred during the October 1987 market crash. For a few days, trading was chaotic in all stocks, large and small, but at least the New York Stock Exchange remained open. However, most emerging growth stocks are traded in the over-the-counter market, which for all practical purposes was closed. No one shut down trading officially; most market makers just stopped answering their phones until the panic dissipated.

These incidents illustrate an inescapable fact of life for emerging growth investors: This sector of the market lacks liquidity and is therefore subject to extreme price volatility, which translates into high transaction costs.

In contrast to emerging growth stocks, large capitalization stocks—Texaco, IBM, Exxon, General Motors, Sears, and the like—are owned in hundreds and hundreds of institutional portfolios and thousands of individual accounts. Even the largest institutional holders don't own more than 1% or 2% of these companies. This breadth of ownership and lack of concentration helps make them extraordinarily liquid. Very large dollar amounts can be bought and sold without any noticeable impact on their price.

Emerging growth stocks are at the other end of the liquidity spectrum. It's quite common to find just a handful of institutional holders owning as much as half of their capitalization. If management also owns a lot of the stock, as is usually the case, then this handful of institutions may control as much as 80% of the stock's float. When one of these large holders decides to sell, he almost always has to take a substantial discount if he wants to get out quickly. Usually the only way for him to avoid driving the stock lower is to be extremely patient, waiting for bids in meaningful size. This may take weeks or even months.

ILLIQUIDITY MEANS VOLATILITY

The over-the-counter market, where the vast majority of emerging growth stocks are traded, is not a centralized market like the New York Stock Exchange. Trading is conducted through brokers who make a market via a computerized telecommunications system. They buy and sell stock for their own accounts to facilitate trading. Inactive stocks may have only one or two market makers, whereas those that trade heavily—Apple Computer and Intel for instance—have a dozen or more market makers. Rather than working on a commission, the market makers earn their revenue on the spread between the bid and asked price. They buy at the lower bid price and sell at the higher asked price. As long as they can match up buyers and sellers, they don't incur any risk. But if they have to hold stock in inventory, there is always a possibility of the price going lower before a buyer turns up. Naturally, this affects their willingness to buy stock for their own account.

It's not uncommon for a large, impatient seller to drive a thinly traded stock down as much as 30%—not because of the mechanics of the over-the-counter market but because of illiquidity. The process begins when the seller gives his order to a market maker, who is usually willing to buy some of the stock for his own account just to let the seller get started. However, if there is no real buyer, other market makers will probably drop their own bids as soon as they see the large offering. They don't want to risk their own capital helping out a competitor. As a result, the stock will drift lower without ever trading in volume—obviously a very frustrating situation.

Often the seller gets impatient and takes the stock to a second market maker. But if there is still no buyer, the stock still won't trade. The only difference is that now there appears to be even more stock for sale, so the other market makers may lower their bids once again. The stock will remain under pressure until a buyer finally turns up or until the seller cancels his orders. Often this doesn't happen until the price is substantially lower than it was when the entire process began. Absolutely nothing about the company has changed—except its stock price, which may be 20% or even 30% lower.

You may wonder how this can happen in a world full of sophisticated institutional investors; what would trigger the kind of impatience responsible for driving a stock 20% or 30% lower? It may be something as innocuous as a personnel change—possibly a new portfolio manager taking over a fund. Or it may be the result of a change in a corporation's pension policy. For instance, many large companies have liquidated their plans as part of restructurings or leveraged buy-outs. When a decision like this is made, responsibility for implementing it is typically assigned to an assistant treasurer. Understandably, he wants to do it as quickly as possible and has little interest in going slow to possibly save an extra point or two.

This kind of illiquidity creates very high transaction costs for institutional investors. If you're an individual investor dealing with a few hundred shares, it's a much less serious problem. But transaction costs are still high. The spread you pay between the bid and the asked price is often greater than the commission on a listed trade. And your broker may tack on a commission anyway, especially if his firm doesn't make a market in the stock. Let's say you're interested in buying a stock that's currently quoted at 10 bid and 10½ asked. This would be a typical spread on a stock that doesn't trade very much; it if were any lower, brokers just wouldn't have enough profit incentive to make a market in it. With a ¼-point commission added, you pay a total of 10¾. But of course, you can't turn around and sell it at that price. With the same spread of ½ point and commission of ¼ point, you don't break even until the bid price goes up to 11. The first 10% earned on your investment goes directly into the broker's pocket. Here's how it works:

	Buy	*Sell*
Bid	10	11
Asked	10½	11½
Your Price	10¾	10¾

Because transaction costs are high for individual and institutional investors alike, it's obviously a good idea to keep portfolio turnover as low as possible. Brokers are the only people who get rich from excessive trading. But sometimes it is possible to use the inherent volatility of emerging growth stocks to your advantage.

TURNING VOLATILITY INTO OPPORTUNITY

Price volatility that's completely unrelated to fundamentals makes most emerging growth investors want to tear their hair out, but it also creates an opportunity to improve performance. This can be done by temporarily overweighting a position. Let's say that 4% of your portfolio is in a particular stock that seems reasonably valued at its current price of $20. Then a large seller comes into the market. There is no buyer around, so the stock comes under pressure, and over a few weeks it drifts down to around 16. On a longer term basis you really don't want more than a 4% position in the stock, but now it appears to be downright cheap instead of just reasonably valued. If you're an institutional investor with the necessary buying power, you might go in and make a bid slightly under the market, at say 15¼, to clean up the seller's entire position. If he hits your bid and the block trades, the stock will probably show some immediate recovery just because there is no longer any supply overhanging the market. Right away you have an unrealized profit. Then as the stock continues to move back up toward the old price of 20, you can gradually lighten up until you get back to the 4% weighting you really wanted all along.

This may sound like a simple, foolproof way to increase a portfolio's return, but it's not. For one thing, the seller could have a larger position than you realized, so the overhang is really not cleaned up after all. This is unlikely if the broker putting together the trade is competent and honest, but it still happens sometimes. A much greater risk is that the seller is basing his action on some new, negative information that you're not yet aware of. When this happens, you're left holding the proverbial bag. It's bad enough that the stock goes down, but being overweighted is like having salt rubbed in your wounds.

The tactic of temporarily overweighting a position is really better suited to institutional investors than individuals. They have the buying power necessary to clean up a large seller, and they also have better access to both trading and fundamental information. If they know the company well and can get through to management, they can be reasonably confident of knowing as much as the seller does. But the risk can never be eliminated completely and should not be taken lightly.

THE SMALL INVESTOR'S EDGE

Although temporarily overweighting a position is a tactic that works best for institutional investors, there are some other trading opportunities that only a small investor can take advantage of. One of these occurred not long ago with a stock that had been publicly traded for only a few months. The broker who had underwritten the public offering also served as the principal market maker. He expected a number of the company's officers to sell stock as soon as possible under Rule 144, which regulates selling by insiders. Anticipating these sales, the broker sold the stock short himself, which put downward pressure on it. He planned to cover his short position at a profit by buying the insiders' stock as soon as it became eligible for sale. But the scheme went awry when the insiders decided they didn't want to sell at the lower price. The broker had to go into the market and bid for stock so he could cover his short position. Naturally this created upward pressure on the stock, and it was soon higher than when the whole episode started.

This entire process took place over a period of a few days, and very little stock actually traded. In fact, the volume was so light that it was impossible for an institutional buyer to take advantage of the lower price. For an individual investor dealing with 1,000 shares or less, however, it was a great opportunity to buy the stock at an artificially depressed price.

Lack of liquidity also creates profit opportunities for individual investors on a longer term basis. These opportunities arise from institutional limitations on capitalization size. Usually institutions don't want to own more than 5% of the outstanding stock of any company. Not only is this an unwieldy amount of stock for them to trade, but it also requires filing with the Securities and Exchange Commission. However, 4% of a company with a $25 million capitalization amounts to only $1 million. And this is too small a position to have a significant impact on most institutional portfolios. In a $200-million mutual fund, for instance, it would be practically lost, representing only ½% of the total assets. So most institutional investors have little interest in companies with capitalizations under $25 million. However, if one of these very small companies grows at 30% or 40%, it will only take a few years for it to reach the institutional-size threshold. If you establish a position early, you may enjoy very high returns when institutional interest eventually does develop.

SELL FIRST, INVESTIGATE LATER

Emerging growth companies run into fundamental problems all the time, and when they do, you want to bail out as fast as possible. This is where individual investors have their most important trading advantage. Unlike institutions, the investor with a small position can sell first and investigate later. For example, let's say a highly regarded small company is expected to report quarterly earnings up 30% from last year, but instead they come in down 40%. As soon as this news hits the tape, the stock will drop like a stone without ever trading. But very quickly it will hit a new equilibrium price. At this point both large and small investors will want to make an assessment of the factors that caused the earnings shortfall; the best place to do it is from the sidelines. But this is feasible only for an investor who owns no more than a few hundred shares. An institutional investor knows that if he sells he will drive the stock lower still, so he wants to be sure of his decision before he pulls the trigger.

When a company reports a significant earnings shortfall, 9 times out of 10 it will be followed by at least one more bad quarter. Some investors refer to this as "the cockroach rule"—the odds of just one bad quarter are about the same as the odds of having just one cockroach. We'll discuss the reasons for this in the next chapter. For now, suffice it to say that even if a company is still fundamentally sound and the problems causing the shortfall really are temporary, it will almost always take more than one quarter to solve them.

Not being constrained by illiquidity, the small investor has the luxury of eliminating his position in the stock and then making an objective and unhurried reassessment of the company's fundamentals. But this option isn't available to the institutional investor whose position is much too large to eliminate without forcing the stock a lot lower still. Before he decides to bail out and take an even bigger loss, he will want to convince himself that the company's problems really are serious and more than just a one- or two-quarter aberration.

The first thing an institutional investor will probably do is check with the analyst who originally recommended the stock to him. This is unlikely to result in a strong negative opinion because analysts have a tendency to turn into unwitting company apologists and, in any event, are naturally reluctant to admit having caused an expensive mistake. Nor is it usually much help to check directly with the company's management. They almost always provide strong assurances that any problem is temporary and well on its way to being remedied, no matter how deep rooted it may be in reality. Few managements are intentionally deceptive or dishonest, but most of them suffer from an overabundance of natural optimism. So the portfolio manager's reluctance to sell the stock is often reinforced by two very biased sources. This creates the institutional inertia that often gives the individual investor an opportunity to bail out of a stock before it goes from bad to worse.

Because of their size and the commission dollars they wield, institutions dominate the trading in most emerging growth stocks. You can count on them receiving the first call from a broker when there is news affecting a stock or when an analyst changes his opinion. There is no escaping this basic fact of life. However, their size also makes it impossible for institutions to be as nimble as an individual investor. In the long run, this freedom to take quick action may outweigh the advantages of size. It's an edge that you shouldn't forefeit through ignorance or neglect.

12

Selling Stocks

It is convenient to talk about emerging growth investing as if it were a step-by-step process that moved from stock selection to valuation and then to trading. But in reality it's an ongoing, continuous activity. At the same time you are searching for and evaluating new companies as portfolio candidates, you must also be pruning out stocks that no longer meet your criteria. Occasionally, a very successful company like Computer Associates will outgrow the emerging growth classification; or, like Spectradyne, it will be bought out. And sometimes a stock should be sold simply because it has become overvalued. Unfortunately, however, disappointing fundamentals are the most common reason for eliminating a holding. But whatever the cause, deciding whether or not to sell a stock is something that emerging growth investors have to deal with continually.

For many investors, selling is the most difficult part of the entire portfolio management process. One thing that makes it so hard is the tendency to forget that you own nothing more than a piece of paper. It's very common to form an emotional attachment to the stocks in your portfolio. I've often seen investors stand in front of a Quotron and root for a stock to go up, much the way bettors at the track root for their horse to run faster. But veteran traders never tire of reminding you of two things:

1. A stock doesn't know you own it.
2. No matter how much you love a stock, it will never love you back.

These wouldn't have become cliches if they weren't true.

In addition to becoming emotionally attached to their stocks, most emerging growth investors are also optimists by nature. They usually think more about a company's potential to grow than about its risks. So when an earnings shortfall occurs, they're often ready to believe it represents a minor problem that can be remedied quickly, rather than a more serious, fundamental weakness. And even after it's become apparent they have made a mistake, they're sometimes still reluctant to admit it, trying to convince themselves that even if their initial assessment was a little off the mark, the stock is now too cheap to sell. In dealing with these very human tendencies that make selling so difficult, it's important to constantly remind yourself that mistakes are an inevitable part of emerging growth investing.

Of course, the best way to minimize the problem of selling is through good stock selection. Obviously, the fewer mistakes you make, the less frequently you will have to sell. Remember to think of yourself as that director of admissions at an Ivy League college. From all of the hundreds of candidates available, you need to choose only a handful to actually own in your portfolio. Certainly there will always be companies in cyclical, low-visibility businesses that have the potential for high returns. But if there is no need to take risks with these kinds of stocks, why do it? An institutional investor may be forced to because of the size of his portfolio. But individual investors don't have to deal with this problem. They can focus exclusively on companies whose high visibility makes them relatively easy to manage and gives them an edge in being able to grow rapidly and still maintain control of their business. The more you use this advantage, the less often you'll face the sell decision.

SELLING RULES

No matter how painstakingly careful you are with stock selection, however, you will still make mistakes and still have to eliminate stocks from time to time. A lot of investors deal with the problem of selling by relying on mechanical rules to make the decision for them. One of these selling tactics entails the use of stop-loss orders. If a stock declines beyond a certain point, say a level 20% below the price at which it was bought, it's automatically sold with no questions asked. You can even give the order to the broker at the same time you buy the stock so you'll be less apt to change your mind if it starts to go down. The appealing part of this strategy is that it theoretically limits the amount of downside risk but doesn't put a cap on the upside potential. However, when it is applied to illiquid emerging growth stocks, it doesn't work nearly as well as it sounds. If a company has stumbled and earnings estimates are being slashed, there is a good chance the stock will fall well below any predetermined price before the first share can be sold. In theory, your downside may be limited to 20%, but if there is no bid for the stock, you'll still own it no matter how much it's down.

A second problem with the stop-loss tactic is that emerging growth stocks sometimes decline because of their lack of liquidity, even when there is no change in fundamentals. As we discussed in the last chapter, this commonly happens when an institutional seller does a sloppy job trying to get out of a large position. If a stock does go down for this reason, a stop-loss rule may trigger a sale just at the very time when you should be thinking in terms of adding to your position. Instead of taking advantage of a buying opportunity, you'll have locked in a loss.

Another common selling discipline is to set a specific objective or target price when you buy a stock. For instance, if you establish a position at an average cost of 20, you might determine ahead of time that you will sell half of it at 28 and eliminate the rest above 32, no matter what. The obvious shortcoming of this strategy is the cap it puts on the stock's upside potential. If a company grows faster than you had expected it to, or the market for its product turns out to be larger than you had originally thought, the stock may actually be a better value today at 28 than it was when you bought it at 20.

In spite of this shortcoming, however, the target price approach to selling does make sense when it's used with cyclical companies that are bought more as trading vehicles than long-term investments. For instance, it's the only way I would consider owning semiconductor or disk drive stocks. Because of their cyclicality and lack of visibility, it's essential to have a specific price objective in mind. Sure, you'll probably end up leaving some money on the table. But this shouldn't hurt performance too much because you want to keep your exposure to this kind of company low anyway. The far bigger risk is that the stock will always look too cheap to sell, and it will be a drag on your portfolio through an entire cycle.

THE RISK OF ELIMINATING WINNERS

The greatest weakness of these mechanical rules or any arbitrary selling discipline, for that matter, is the risk of eliminating a winner prematurely. As you know by now, there are many ways that small, fast-growing companies can run into fundamental problems and stumble badly. No matter how much care you dedicate to the stock selection process, you will inevitably make some disappointing investments. It's simply part of the nature of emerging growth investing. Only by holding onto your winners can you overcome these mistakes and earn enough extra return to make the above-average risk of emerging growth stocks worth taking on. But a sure way of not getting the maximum possible mileage out of your winners is to sell them out because of an arbitrary rule.

Similarly, you should be cautious about eliminating a stock from your portfolio for no reason other than valuation. The range of returns between good performers and bad ones always seems to be much greater than you ever expect. Companies with strong momentum have a way of doing better than you had ever hoped, just as those with disappointing fundamentals commonly turn out a little worse than had seemed possible. As we discussed earlier, companies with expanding margins usually have earnings that come in ahead of analysts' estimates. As a result, they often gain increased recognition, and investors bid their P/E ratios up to higher levels. This combination of factors turns them into home-run stocks, leveraging their returns way above anyone's expectations. Yet in hindsight, their performance always seems quite reasonable. So never be too anxious to sell a stock just because you have a big profit in it. It may still have a long way to go.

One of the greatest winners ever owned by the New Horizons Fund was Wal-Mart Stores. This Arkansas-based retailer compiled an extraordinary record of earnings growth by opening store after store in small-town markets that other chains ignored. Here is a comment made at the fund's 1982 annual meeting, 12 years after it had made its initial purchase of Wal-Mart shares:

> We first purchased the stock in 1970. Over the past two years, New Horizons has realized a capital gain of over $15 million in Wal-Mart. Even so, as of March 31, 1982, it was the Fund's largest holding, with a market value of over $22 million. The stock price at the end of March was $45.75 per share, and our cost basis on the shares held is $2.51. Clearly Wal-Mart has been a most successful investment and one which epitomizes our approach. New Horizons identified the company early, has remained a shareholder for a long period, and has profited handsomely from the company's superior growth record.

Obviously, there were times during this 12-year span when Wal-Mart seemed to be fully valued. But New Horizons only trimmed its position; it never eliminated it. So it captured a lot of the original investment's 1,700% plus price appreciation. Holding on to a winner of this magnitude can offset a lot of mistakes.

If a company's fundamentals are as strong as ever and the stock's valuation is your only worry, your best move is probably to sell just part of your position. Let's say that when you first bought a stock it represented 5% of your portfolio, but it has done so well that now it's up to 10%. Even though it seems fully priced on a near-term basis, you may be better off just cutting it back to the original 5% weighting instead of eliminating it altogether. This way you can nail down a good profit and still maintain your original exposure. And having already sold some at a higher price, you'll be much more likely to buy the stock again if it eventually comes back down.

RED FLAGS

Although mechanical rules may be of dubious value, there are some other more general and less arbitrary principles that can help make you a better seller. To start, you should always be alert for the red flags that sometimes signal an early warning of disappointing fundamentals. Among the most common are accounting changes. More than one emerging growth company has kept its earnings on track by changing the way it keeps the books. For instance, it may start to capitalize an item that it had always expensed. Or it may liberalize its depreciation schedules. Or it may reverse part of an earlier accrual. Liberalizing the criteria for recognizing a sale is another way of inflating sales and earnings.

Naturally, there will always be a logical explanation for this kind of change, and sometimes it will be valid. But often the real reason will be to cover up a deterioration in fundamentals, in hopes that it can be remedied quickly. Another way of doing this is by accruing for taxes at a lower rate. So you should always check a company's growth rate on both a pretax and aftertax basis.

Something else to look out for is a big increase in accounts receivable. For instance, if sales grow by 25% and receivables are up 45%, it's possible the company is offering a lot of special incentives to close sales. This can become a problem if sales are really being borrowed from future periods; it will make the upcoming comparisons that much more difficult.

ACQUISITIONS

Acquisitions are another red flag to stay alert for. They don't always spell trouble, but they make me nervous because they're often a sign that growth is slowing down. Managements frequently think that acquiring another company is the easiest way and maybe the only way to achieve their growth targets and satisfy investors' expectations. But they don't usually succeed. Often acquisitions distract management at just the time when the original business needs attention the most. At the very least, they make the company bigger and more complex and therefore more difficult to control. This alone increases the risk that it will stumble and produce an earnings shortfall. But in addition, the acquired company's weaknesses frequently turn out to be more severe than anticipated, and getting it in shape often requires more attention and support than is possible. So instead of helping to sustain growth, the acquisition actually turns out to be a drain.

Of course, not all acquisitions represent a desperate attempt to sustain growth. Sometimes they're just a convenient shortcut for achieving another goal. This was the case with Healthcare Services Group, a fine little company that compiled a record of consistent growth—right up until it made its first acquisition.

Healthcare is in a rather unglamorous business: It provides housekeeping and linen services to nursing homes. By concentrating on just this one market niche, it has developed an expertise that enables it to deliver its service for less than nursing-home operators can do it themselves. It also does a better job. And in the process it earns a respectable profit for its shareholders.

Healthcare has contracts with all of its clients, but these can be canceled on 30-days' notice. Therefore, its revenue is recurring only as long as it continues to provide good service, but over the years its clients have renewed at better than a 95% rate. So practically every new contract it wins does represent incremental revenue.

The company has grown by repeating over and over the same thing it has done since the day it was started—convincing nursing-home operators that it can save them money and management headaches and then doing it. Through this process, it has gradually extended its geographic operating area out from its Philadelphia base. The cookie-cutter simplicity of the business, combined with its good visibility, helped Healthcare to compile an excellent earnings record—up until the time it tried to accelerate its growth with an acquisition. Healthcare had always planned to enter the New England market and when a company already operating in that area became available, it saw the acquisition as an opportunity to speed up the process. It also thought it would avoid the startup losses normally incurred with a move into a new geographic market.

All of this was very appealing in theory. However, the acquired company turned out to have a few flaws that hadn't been obvious before the deal was closed. None of them were critical, but they did require some

serious management attention. Unfortunately, Healthcare, itself, didn't
have enough management depth to deal with them quickly. So for several
quarters earnings comparisons were unfavorable, and the stock's performance reflected the disappointing results.

Healthcare's experience is all too typical. Any company growing at a
rate of 30% or higher is operating under considerable strain, and the
chances are good that its management is already stretched thin. An acquisition will just add to the strain and stretch management even thinner.
And 9 times out of 10, the acquired company will turn out to have some
weaknesses or problems that hadn't been apparent until it was too late. It
may be possible to straighten them out eventually, but in the meantime
some other part of the company's operations will probably run into
trouble. Management ends up spending all of its time putting out fires
instead of positioning the company to grow, and soon it loses its momentum. Healthcare was fortunate because it was able to keep the problem
isolated from the rest of the company, and eventually it resumed its
growth. But a lot of companies are never able to regain their momentum.

I get particularly nervous about acquisitions when the company making them, like Healthcare, has had little or no experience in this area. By
contrast, Computer Associates has relied on them heavily in achieving its
excellent growth and by now certainly knows what it is doing. This company has always looked to acquisitions as an important source of new
products that its sales force can market to the existing customer base. Because its real interest is in acquiring products, not companies, it never
wastes time in slashing costs to the bone as it rolls the acquired company's
operations into its own.

Computer Associates' success shows that acquisitions aren't always a
prelude to disaster. But because it's had plenty of experience evaluating
them, it knows how to make a realistic assessment of the resources an
acquisition will demand, as well as the profit it will contribute. This is
considerably different from the typical emerging growth company that
looks at acquisitions only occasionally. All too often these companies un-
derestimate the problems that will inevitably accompany an acquisition
and overestimate their ability to deal with them.

THE PRIVATE COMPANY MENTALITY

Another, more subtle red flag has to do with management attitude: Some
public companies are run as if they were privately owned. This problem is
seldom obvious, but I've encountered it on more than one occasion. Companies that are affected by it don't always experience a severe earnings

shortfall. Instead, their earnings just fail to grow as fast as they should. Management usually explains, in very statesmanlike terms, that it's acting to maximize long-term growth, even if this requires some short-term sacrifice. They imply that to be any more concerned with short-term results would really be nearsighted, if not downright irresponsible.

When this problem occurs, it's typically with older companies that have been in business for a number of years prior to public ownership. Usually the founder still owns the majority of the stock and has no reason to fear a hostile tender offer. Probably his main reason for taking the company public in the first place was to gain personal liquidity and provide for his estate. Access to equity capital to finance future growth was really a secondary consideration. As a result, he runs the business as if it were still privately held, and he shows very little regard for the interest of the public shareholders.

These turn out to be disappointing investments when the founder/ CEO is more interested in making the company a monument to himself than maximizing its earnings growth. Usually companies like this have a very profitable core business. But the core business doesn't receive the attention and nurturing it needs to realize its full potential; instead, its profits are used as a source of financing for other ventures. Too many resources—in terms of both money and management effort—are pumped into marginal new ventures, which not only dilute the growth of the core business but may also weaken it.

In theory the outside directors should protect the public shareholders from this happening. But they are usually old friends or business associates of the founder. In addition, they own much less stock and know much less about the company's operations than he does. So they probably won't have much influence, especially if earnings progress is not really bad, but just below the company's potential.

You won't always lose money with a company like this, but they inevitably give you more than your fair share of frustration.

PULLING THE TRIGGER

Unfortunately, when an emerging growth company runs into trouble, most of the time you won't have any of these early warnings. On the contrary, it's much more likely that your first indication will be the actual announcement of an earnings shortfall. When this happens, the stock will inevitably experience immediate selling pressure. If you're a natural optimist—as many emerging growth investors are—you'll probably look for a plausible explanation of why the problem is temporary. You may even conclude that the market has overreacted and the downward pressure on the stock has created an unusual buying opportunity. You may be tempted to add to your position in the stock. *But this will be the wrong way to react practically every time. You will be much better served if you respond to disappointing fundamentals by selling, and selling ruthlessly.*

There are times to be patient. But this isn't one of them, especially if you're an individual investor with a small enough position to get out of the stock without putting further downward pressure on it.

WHY BAD NEWS USUALLY FOLLOWS BAD NEWS

Over the years, I have heard of disappointing quarters blamed on everything from a series of incredibly unlucky breaks to bad weather. These excuses are nearly always very plausible but are usually misleading. When an emerging growth company experiences a significant decline in quarterly earnings, it's more often because of a fundamental problem. And it takes a while to just define most problems, let alone solve them. So usually one bad quarter is followed by another and then another.

Once a problem has been identified and defined, actually solving it may entail a significant change in the company's organizational structure or a modification of its product or service. It may also be necessary to recruit a key executive to oversee the part of the business causing the problem. None of these things can be done quickly. And in the meantime, because management's attention is focused on the problem area, some other aspect of the business is often neglected and gets out of control. As this is happening, morale may decline and cause further problems. People who thought they were working for a company whose growth would create nothing but opportunities now find themselves worrying about job security. Stock options that had looked like the basis for financial security are suddenly worth much less. Changes like this don't make for happy employees. And the company's credibility with its customer base may also suffer. As we saw earlier, this was certainly a large part of Hogan Systems' problems.

The following excerpt* from a *Wall Street Journal* (3/1/88, p. 6) article illustrates some typical problems of the type that aren't likely to be resolved quickly. The subject is LyphoMed, a generic drug company that compiled a very impressive growth record until it encountered quality control trouble, a problem often associated with high growth.

LyphoMed Inc. was one of the golden generic drug companies, but its luster of late has been dulled by a spate of problems—manufacturing, pricing, and regulatory—now compounded by legal woes.

Carving out a profitable generic niche as a supplier of injectable drugs to hospitals, Rosemont, Ill.-based LyphoMed's earnings since it went public in 1983 have grown ninefold to $21 million, or 70 cents a share, on sales of $172.7 million in 1987. It gained a more humane image by developing pentamidine, a drug for AIDS-related pneumonia, as its first exclusive product.

Now, however, LyphoMed is saddled with a product recall and regulatory reprimands for having sold adulterated goods and violated "good manufacturing practices" of the Food and Drug Administration. As a result, the FDA has frozen the company's applications to sell any new drugs made in its Chicago-area plants, pending completion of an agency inspection. Separately, the company has been hit by allegations of "profiteering" after it quadrupled the price of pentamidine to $100 a vial from $25. . . .

Between February and July last year, an FDA investigator, John Bruederle, visited LyphoMed's Ruby Street plant in Melrose Park, Ill., and discovered a panoply of problems, according to his report. Vials of antibiotics and steroids to treat inflammation were filled below the dose level claimed on the label. The "lyophilizer," a machine used to freeze-dry drugs, was contaminated but the company failed to perform a required follow-up test to determine why.

The FDA also says the company started shipping two products, pentamidine for acquired immune deficiency syndrome and an antibiotic, from a new plant before it got the FDA approval needed for such a manufacturing change. Indeed, the shipments occurred even before the applications were filed. . . .

What caused LyphoMed's quality problems that the FDA cited is a point of debate. "They grew too fast," says Leonard Yaffee, an analyst at Montgomery Securities in San Francisco. "They outstripped their internal controls. They had too many products going out the door to be able to do the job they should have."

Some past and current employees agree. Quality-control staffing didn't keep pace with production increases, and a "hot list" of urgent tasks overwhelmed long range planning and training. . . .

When this news broke, it wasn't clear how severe an impact these problems would have on LyphoMed's earnings. But it was a good bet that they would take some time to remedy. Even if the company could cure its quality-control deficiencies quickly, there would still be questions about its credibility with the hospitals that bought its products, its relationship with the FDA, and the morale of its employees—all of which would probably take more than a quarter or two to restore. Not surprisingly, a few weeks later, LyphoMed reported a down quarter, and the quarter after that it showed a $15-million loss.

PRUNING YOUR PORTFOLIO

When a company does encounter fundamental problems, its stock will usually come under increasing pressure as one disappointing quarter follows another. By being quick to sell, you may be able to avoid the full extent of the decline. And even if the stock makes a bottom quickly, washing out most of the risk, you still have the prospect of dead money. As long as the company continues to struggle, the stock won't have much upside either. Unless you pull the trigger quickly, you'll end up with a portfolio that is loaded down with too much deadwood—stocks that just sit there without ever moving either up or down very much.

This is an insidious problem because it saps your portfolio of vitality. To realize the promise of the emerging growth style of investing, you need plenty of fresh ideas. You need a portfolio full of companies that will have superior earnings growth and that have home-run potential. One way of being sure that you have this kind of portfolio and not one full of dead wood is to have a quick trigger finger when it comes to selling stocks whose fundamentals are turning sour.

Part IV
From Theory to Practice

13

Profiles in Growth

Discussing an investment strategy in theory is one thing; actually putting it into practice is quite another. In this chapter we'll prepare for that critical step by analyzing some specific companies. Although they operate in different industries, all five of these companies meet the stock selection criteria we discussed earlier, and, what is important is they all have good visibility. This provides a tremendous advantage: It makes them relatively easy businesses to run and greatly reduces the chance that they'll get out of control.

But keep in mind that visibility only increases the odds of sustaining a high growth rate; it's not an ironclad guarantee. The fundamentals of emerging growth companies often change quickly. So it would be dangerous to interpret these case studies as stock recommendations.

Of necessity, our analysis will deal with these companies strictly as businesses rather than as stocks. As we discussed earlier, it's important to distinguish between the two. After all, the greatest growth companies in the world won't be very good investments if you buy their stocks at inflated prices. Here we'll only be talking about the companies, not the stocks.

NEW ENGLAND CRITICAL CARE

For someone who is seriously ill, the best place to be is usually a hospital. But hospitals are full of sick people, so for some they're also the worst possible place to be. An AIDS victim, for instance, could be exposed to a wide variety of potentially fatal infectious diseases in a hospital setting. For this kind of patient, the home provides a much safer environment for treatment.

AIDS victims are among the thousands of seriously ill people who make up the home infusion therapy market, which New England Critical Care serves. Home infusion therapy didn't come into existence until the late 1970s, but today it's well on the way to becoming a $1-billion business. It started with parenteral nutrition, a technique by which patients who have little or no digestive tract function are fed nutrients through a surgically implanted catheter. This particular segment still accounts for well over half of the industry's total revenue. Less important but still significant is enteral nutrition therapy for patients with partial digestive tract function. But the fastest growing part of the industry is home antibiotic therapy, which can be used to treat over 20 different types of conditions, such as infections of the kidneys and urinary tract. Other services include chemotherapy, pain management, and treatment for congestive heart failure.

New England Critical Care provides these services through a network of regional centers, all of which are equipped with a sterile "clean room," where the company's own registered pharmacists prepare all medications and nutritional solutions. Many of these compounds are custom-tailored to be "patient-specific." The regional centers are also staffed with registered nurses, who are the focal point for patient care. They visit the patients regularly, work closely with their families, and provide training in I-V use. Other center employees include patient service representatives, reimbursement specialists, and business managers. Contrary to what its name implies, the company's geographic scope extends as far south as Atlanta and as far west as Salt Lake City.

Some industry analysts expect home infusion therapy to grow at a 30%–35% rate into the early 1990s and believe that home antibiotic therapy, the segment in which New England Critical Care is particularly strong, will grow at an even faster rate. The favorable industry prognosis is the result of several important trends that are affecting practically every aspect of health care. To start, a dominant force in all health care today is cost containment. After years of unabated inflation in the cost of delivering medical services, both government and industry have taken strong steps to put a lid on these costs. For instance, Medicare reimbursement to hospitals is no longer based on the cost of treatment. Instead, it's paid out according to a system of diagnosis-related groups (DRGs). Under DRGs a hospital is reimbursed the same amount for an appendectomy, whether the patient is discharged after 3 days or 8. As a result of this change, hospitals are paying a lot more attention to costs, and are sending many patients home earlier.

Another development that reflects the new emphasis on cost containment is the rapid growth in health maintenance organization (HMO) membership. Because members prepay a fixed fee that covers all their health care needs, the doctors and administrators who run these programs have a strong incentive to minimize costs within the bounds of proper care. So HMOs, like DRGs, represent a powerful force at work to shorten the length of hospital stays. This obviously means that more patients, and sicker patients, must be treated outside of the hospital—a trend that clearly benefits the home infusion therapy business.

New technology is also having a positive impact on the growth of home infusion therapy. This is most apparent in the sharp increase in the number of medical problems that can now be treated in the home environment. Just a few years ago, the market was limited to patients with digestive tract problems. Today it has expanded to include people suffering from cancer, AIDS, and other infectious diseases. And this expansion is likely to continue because many of the new drugs being developed by the biotechnology industry are particularly well suited for home delivery. Much as Spectradyne benefited from the availability of cheaper and more powerful semiconductors, New England Critical Care stands to benefit from new technology developed by other companies.

Still another force that's promoting the rapid growth of home therapy is its life-style advantage. Even though they cost more than a five-star hotel, most hospitals are not very pleasant places to stay. Not only does home therapy make it possible for the patient to return to a more pleasant environment sooner, it also enables him or her to resume a more normal way of living. Many patients, for instance, are able to return to work while still being treated. This often has a positive psychological impact that helps their recovery.

Cost containment pressures, new technology, and life-style benefits are three important trends that should allow home infusion therapy to remain a high-growth industry. And New England Critical Care may be able to grow even faster than the industry as a whole because it's particularly strong in antibiotic therapy, the fastest-growing market segment. It also has the opportunity to augment its growth by expanding into new geographic markets.

Like all rapidly growing companies, New England Critical Care faces the challenge of keeping its growth under control, but in this regard it has several important advantages. First, there is a strong repeat element to its business. Many patients continue to receive home therapy for months or years, some even for the rest of their lives. For all practical purposes, this

TABLE 13.1 New England Critical Care Financial Summary ($000s omitted)

Year Ending 12/31	1985	1986	1987
Revenue	$12,377	$21,087	$31,318
Operating Margin	Negative	16.8%	16.5%
Operating Income	(435)	3,548	5,164
Interest and Other Income, Net	(73)	(78)	736
Tax	—	1,585	2,360
Net Income from Operations	$ (508)	$ 1,885	$ 3,539
Earnings per Share	$(.17)	$.51	$.69
Long-Term Debt	$ 1,808	$ 219	$ 182
Equity	4,387	18,049	44,433
Return on Average Equity	Negative	16.8%	11.3%
Operating Cash Flow	$ (17)	$ 2,493	$ 4,558
Working Capital Increase	5,582	1,500	2,874
Capital Expenditures	706	1,018	1,770
Surplus/(Deficit)	$ (6,305)	$ (25)	$ (86)

provides the company with a significant base of recurring revenue. In addition, it has all the advantages commonly associated with a service business—closeness to the customer, ability to compete on more than just the basis of price, low capital intensity, and no inventory cycles to contend with.

New England Critical Care's primary risk is that as it expands into new geographic markets, it will inevitably face some stiff competition, particularly from Caremark. This fine company, which merged with Baxter-Travenol in 1987, is several times larger. And its management believes the merger will allow it to expand more aggressively. If New England Critical Care goes toe to toe with Caremark in too many local markets or trys to expand too rapidly, there's a good chance that it will stumble. So far, however, the company seems willing to accept more moderate growth as the price of keeping its business under control. This is certainly an encouraging sign.

THE MACNEAL-SCHWENDLER CORPORATION

The engineer whose job is designing a critical part for a jet engine faces a tough challenge. On one hand he must keep the part as light as possible;

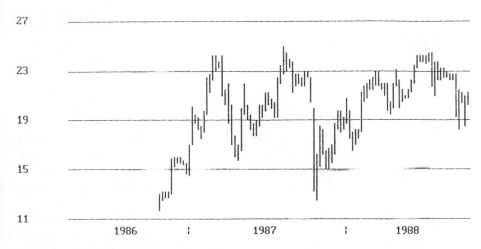

Figure 13.1. New England Critical Care, Inc. stock chart. Courtesy of Bridge Information Systems, Inc.

on the other, he has to make sure it's strong enough to function reliably. The traditional approach to resolving this weight/strength trade-off was to build a prototype of the part and subject it to physical testing. The engineer would take the test results and go back to the drawing board to improve on the original design and then test once more—repeating the cycle until at last he came up with a design that met his criteria for both weight and strength. The process was long, tedious, and expensive.

Today this traditional approach to solving mechanical engineering problems is well on its way to becoming obsolete because of computer-aided engineering (CAE). This technology enables an engineer to actually analyze a prototype design without physically manufacturing it. In addition to saving considerable time and money, CAE also increases design flexibility. For instance, the engineer designing the critical jet engine part can use CAE to analyze the stress distribution of his design. This allows him to remove material from areas where stress is low and add it to areas where stress is high. The information provided by CAE makes it possible to design aircraft that are both stronger and lighter.

The MacNeal-Schwendler Corporation is the dominant supplier of CAE software for mechanical engineers. Its principal product, a program called MSC/NASTRAN, was originally developed for NASA. So, as you would expect, major clients include companies like Boeing, McDonnell-Douglas, Grumman, and General Dynamics. However, MacNeal-Schwendler has also cultivated a number of new markets so that its software is now used in a much broader spectrum of applications. For instance, most major automobile manufacturers use it to analyze components from engine blocks to transmissions. It has also been used in designing products as diverse as intraocular lenses, 12-meter America's Cup yachts, cameras, tractors, photo copiers, and artificial hip joints.

MacNeal-Schwendler's principal product, which is descended from a government-owned program, was first brought out in 1971. By high-tech standards, this is ancient. But the original version has been replaced more than 65 times, so today's version bears no more resemblance to the original than a Ford Taurus does to a Model T. In addition to constantly refining and upgrading its software, MacNeal-Schwendler has also adapted it to run on more than 25 different combinations of computers and operating systems.

By concentrating virtually all of its efforts on just this one market niche, MacNeal-Schwendler has been able to establish a very strong, well-entrenched competitive position. In fact, its product has become so much of a standard that computer manufacturers have actually modified new designs to accommodate it. For a competitor to develop a similar program would be expensive and probably take 3 to 5 years. And then it would have to overcome the fact that MSC/NASTRAN is an industry standard that engineers already know how to use and are confident with.

To solidify its competitive position even more, MacNeal-Schwendler follows a marketing strategy a lot like that of the nineteenth-century missionaries, who recognized that if they could convert children, they would have them for life. By making its programs available to over 100 universities at very low cost, MacNeal-Schwendler can be certain that tomorrow's engineers will be users of its software right from the start of their training.

MacNeal-Schwendler is different from most of the companies in its industry because instead of selling its software under a perpetual license, it leases it on a monthly basis. This policy provides a stream of revenue that's very close to 100% recurring, so there is very good visibility for planning and managing the business. Interestingly, the monthly lease payments are based on usage, subject to a specified minimum. And almost every client increases his usage over time as he becomes increasingly familiar with the program. As shown here, this trend has caused the company's revenue to consistently grow at a faster pace than its installed base:

Year	Average Installations	Percentage Change	Revenue	Percentage Change
1984	363	23.1%	$11,801	28.0%
1985	442	21.8	15,334	29.9
1986	544	23.1	21,101	37.6
1987	660	21.3	27,078	28.3
1988	780	18.3	34,530	27.5

Besides providing the basis for a recurring revenue stream, the leasing policy also promotes close customer relations. Because the revenue stream depends on usage, there is a lot of incentive to provide new clients with plenty of training and support, and to keep in touch with older clients by offering them consulting services. In addition to maximizing revenue, this also helps MacNeal-Schwendler maintain its strong competitive position and keep its technology state-of-the-art. Here's how the company describes its philosophy in this regard:

> Although MSC/NASTRAN is MSC's principal product, our principal offering to our clients is service. Our responsibility to our clients does not end when we ship a magnetic computer tape to them—it is only the beginning. Throughout the relationship, we strive to
>
> - Offer a product that is as error-free as possible. We take great pains to make this a reality through excellence in design and extensive quality assurance testing.
>
> - Assist our users to use our products. Part of this responsibility is to design in as many "ease-of-use" features as we can. Another part is to be constantly ready to answer questions regarding product usage. . . . Still another part of this responsibility is training.
>
> - Provide our clients with products that contain state-of-the-art, proven software and engineering technology. This responsibility must be met two ways. First, we must always listen to our clients to assess their needs and incorporate those needs as best we can into our products. Second, we must lead our clients into new technologies through our research and development efforts.

As it attempts to extend its growth into the future, MacNeal-Schwendler will have some important advantages working in its favor. First, the recurring revenue base provides a marvelous cushion, so that when the number of new placements declines, revenue can still increase. Second, the policy of basing lease payments on usage provides another avenue for growth. In fact, much of the company's development spending is directed to programs that complement MSC/NASTRAN and are intended to increase its usage.

And finally, the basic market itself has plenty of potential to grow larger. The market was once limited to large corporations but is now being opened up to other users. Because small, inexpensive computers have become more powerful, a mainframe or minicomputer is no longer required to run MacNeal-Schwendler's software. Modified versions are now available for use on engineering workstations and even personal computers. Thus the system's economics are coming within the reach of more and more potential users.

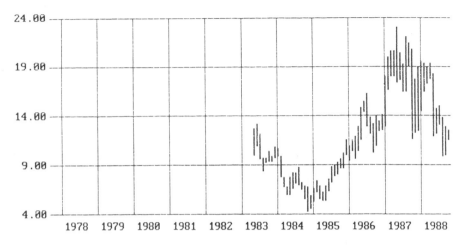

Figure 13.2. MacNeal–Schwendler Corporation stock chart. Courtesy of Bridge Information Systems, Inc.

Because its product is so proprietary, MacNeal-Schwendler's pricing structure allows it excellent profitability. Its pretax operating margins have exceeded 40%, and its return on equity has been close to 30% (see Table 13.2). With no need for expensive inventory or physical plant, the business is not at all capital-intensive. Therefore, the company has been able to maintain an exceedingly strong balance sheet—lots of cash and short term-investments, a current ratio in excess of 5:1, and essentially zero debt. At the same time, it has been able to support a dividend payout ratio of over 25%—very high in the world of emerging growth.

Ironically, these superb financial characteristics are also a cause for concern. Clearly, MacNeal-Schwendler generates a lot more cash than it needs to support its own growth, so it can also finance acquisitions with ease. Unfortunately, its last foray into this area turned out quite badly. During its 1985 fiscal year, MacNeal-Schwendler purchased a 35% stake in another small software company and just the following year wrote off the entire investment because of continuing losses. With good reason, another acquisition attempt is bound to encounter a lot of shareholder skepticism.

Another concern that bothers some investors is the amount of software development cost that the company capitalizes. Prior to its 1987 fiscal year, MacNeal-Schwendler followed the conservative accounting policy of expensing all its research and development. However, Statement 86, a new standard issued by the Financial Accounting Standards Board, forced all software companies to abandon this method. So in fiscal 1987, MacNeal-Schwendler capitalized slightly more than 50% of its development costs for

TABLE 13.2 MacNeal-Schwendler Corp. Financial Summary ($000s omitted)

Year Ending 1/31	1986	1987	1988
Revenue	$21,101	$27,078	$34,530
Operating Margin	37.2%	43.2%	40.9%
Operating Income	7,844	11,692	14,114
Interest and Other Income, Net	544	1,000	1,001
Tax	3,522	5,687	6,046
Net Income from Operations	$ 4,866	$ 7,005	$ 9,069
Earning per Share	$.40	$.58	$.74
Long-Term Debt	$ 33	$ —	$ —
Equity	21,301	27,217	34,448
Return on Average Equity	23.6%	28.9%	29.4%
Operating Cash Flow	$ 5,556	$ 9,164	$11,303
Working Capital Increase	984	788	(516)
Capital Expenditures	2,797	4,018	6,990
Surplus/(Deficit)	$ 1,775	$ 4,358	$ 4,829

amortization against future revenue. Some critics pointed out this was a high percentage relative to other software companies. However, considering that almost all of these costs were directed at supporting MSC/NASTRAN, the amount capitalized was probably a lot more reasonable than it may have appeared at first glance. At any rate, this criticism and the concern about acquisitions seem quite minor in comparison to the outstanding attributes that are working in MacNeal-Schwendler's favor.

PCS, INC.

If the place where you work offers a health plan that includes reimbursement for prescription drugs, there is a good chance you're one of more than 8 million PCS cardholders. With one of these cards, you can walk into 9 out of 10 pharmacies and have your prescription filled for a fee of only a dollar or two. The participating pharmacies, which number 60,000, send the claim back to PCS's headquarters. After checking it out via more than 50 verification steps, the company sends out a check to reimburse the pharmacy for the wholesale cost of the drug, plus a dispensing fee. The cycle is completed when PCS itself is reimbursed by the plan sponsor. For providing this service, PCS charges a small fee—well under $1 per prescription.

The Prescription Card System, as the service is called, has a lot of appeal for both participating companies and their employees. It saves the employee the hassle of having to submit forms for reimbursement, and it saves the employer money. For instance, under a major medical plan the total claim cost for a prescription is $25 to $30. By comparison, the same cost for a claim processed by PCS is $18 to $19. Of this total, about 78% represents the cost of the drug, 18% is the fee paid to the dispensing pharmacist, and the remaining 4% is PCS's fee for processing the claim.

There are two reasons why such significant savings are possible with the PCS program. First, PCS has the computing power and the organizational setup to process millions of prescription claims quickly and efficiently. This results in a substantial cost advantage relative to a system that is designed primarily for processing major medical claims. Second, PCS's representation of large, cohesive numbers of pharmacy customers creates bargaining power for plan sponsors, much the way an organized labor union gives its collective members leverage that would be unattainable by any individual worker. As a result, the plan sponsors' reimbursement cost is considerably less than the regular retail price of the drug.

Historically, PCS's largest clients have been insurance companies, who sell the service to employers as part of an overall medical insurance package. The client base also includes a number of Blue Cross/Blue Shield organizations, HMOs, preferred provider organizations, and labor unions, as well as companies that administer their own employee plans. Because PCS has long-term relationships with these sponsors and is paid a fee for each transaction, of which there are well over a million in an average week, it enjoys a very stable stream of recurring revenue.

PCS also has the advantage of operating in an industry environment that is very conducive to growth. To start, it benefits from the same health care containment forces that have helped New England Critical Care. As you can see from the data shown here, cardholder growth picked up substantially in 1985 and has accelerated since then. To a large degree this has been attributable to the company's marketing emphasis on the cost-containment aspect of its service.

Year	Cardholders (000s)	Percentage Change
1983	2331	4%
1984	2565	10
1985	3237	26
1986	4391	36
1987	6088	39
1988	7700	27

Notwithstanding PCS's strong growth, its penetration of the potential market is still quite low, and saturation is not likely to become a problem anytime in the near future. In the 1987 Annual Report, the company's CEO noted that "if PCS's cardholder base were to increase 30% annually for the next five years, the company would have only 33% of the potential market."

Another factor that should help the company to continue growing is its very strong competitive position. Not only is PCS a clear leader with limited competition, but the barriers to entering its business are formidable. Before offering a competitive service, a new entrant would first have to make substantial investments in computer equipment and software and then establish relationships with thousands of pharmacies.

Given PCS's well-entrenched competitive position, it's no surprise that it has healthy profit margins and an extremely high return on equity (see Table 13.3). However, it has been able to achieve its excellent profitability without significant price increases and in spite of the low cost of its service. In this regard, an important help has been the fact that a lot of its costs are relatively fixed, so the incremental profit from new cardholders carries very high margins. This characteristic also shows up in a pattern of expanding profit margins that PCS experienced through 1987. However, this favorable trend was interrupted, at least temporarily, in 1988 by relatively high startup costs associated with a big increase in capital spending.

Much of this money was spent on a new magnetic card reading system, called Recap, which will bring claims processing on-line and allow direct communication between PCS and the pharmacist while the prescrip-

TABLE 13.3 PCS, Inc. Financial Summary

Year Ending 3/31	1986	1987	1988
Revenue	$39,400	$54,456	$76,742
Operating Margin	25.8%	28.9%	26.2%
Operating Income	10,174	15,741	20,124
Amortization of Intangibles and Minority Interest	108	373	241
Tax	5,058	7,684	8,306
Net Income from Operations	$ 5,008	$ 7,684	$11,577
Earnings per Share	$.35	$.53	$.80
Long-Term Debt	—	—	—
Equity	$ 7,669	$13,334	$25,315
Return on Average Equity	68.3%	80.4%	63.1%
Operating Cash Flow	$ 6,790	$10,603	$16,051
Working Capital Increase	989	(12,051)	(16,778)
Capital Expenditures	1,845	2,814	12,600
Surplus/(Deficit)	$ 3,956	$19,841	$20,229

tion is being filled. The new system, which the company calls the key to the future, will include several important features. Primary among these is greater flexibility: It will give PCS plan sponsors almost unlimited ability to tailor their prescription drug plans. For instance, the pharmacist will now know immediately whether an annual deductible has been met and whether a generic alternative may be substituted in filling the prescription. This added flexibility will further enhance PCS's appeal to potential plan sponsors and should be an important marketing point. Another advantage of the on-line system is that it will further buttress the company's already strong competitive position. Eventually, it should also result in substantial savings through the reduction of data entry and other costs. In this regard, it's reminiscent of Paychex's program to upgrade its data-processing capability. You have to suspect that once the system is fully installed and the startup costs are out of the way, it may lead to the same kind of margin expansion.

Another aspect of PCS's business, which is a natural outgrowth of its data-gathering activities, is its Pharmaceutical Data Services. This unit sells research on the use patterns of prescription drugs to major pharmaceutical manufacturers. Although the company's competitive position is not nearly as strong in this area, it is nonetheless an attractive, proprietary service business that could represent an avenue of continued growth once market saturation eventually becomes an issue for the prescription card service.

Prior to its initial public offering in November 1986, PCS was wholly owned by McKesson, a wholesale pharmaceutical distribution company. McKesson continues to own about 85% of the stock and has effective control of PCS. This bothers some investors because of the potential for conflicts of interest. For instance, PCS has agreed not to enter the mail-order retail drug business, in part because it would be awkward for McKesson to compete with its customers through PCS. However, this is a small concern relative to the many strengths that should help PCS to extend its record of growth.

SUNGARD DATA SYSTEMS

It seems that 9 out of 10 people who work in an office spend the better part of their day sitting in front of a screen—either the monitor on a personal computer or a terminal tied into a larger system. Of course, this is a reflection of how dependent most businesses are on their data-processing systems to keep track of all their daily transactions. PCS is just one example

Figure 13.3. PCS, Inc. stock chart. Courtesy of Bridge Information Systems, Inc.

of a company that couldn't operate without its computer systems. Banks, airlines, and hundreds of other businesses fall into the same category. An uninterrupted flow of data is no less vital to these companies than is an uninterrupted flow of oxygen to a living creature.

This absolute dependence on computers is the foundation for disaster recovery services, a business pioneered by SunGard Data Systems. It functions much like an insurance policy for large-scale computer users. If a subscriber's system goes down, he transfers his data-processing function to one of SunGard's facilities and may continue to use it for up to 90 days while he brings his own system back on line. Of course, most sophisticated computer users take elaborate precautions of their own to protect themselves from losing data or computing power. But some events are impossible to guard against—fires, floods, and earthquakes, for instance. During 1987 one or more SunGard subscribers experienced each of these three types of disasters, and in every case their computer capabilities were quickly restored.

To back up its subscribers, SunGard maintains very large-scale facilities—called disaster recovery centers—in Philadelphia, Chicago, and San Diego. These centers form the three main hubs in a nationwide telecommunications network that allows the customer's remote locations to access SunGard's computers. The network also makes it possible for customers to test or use the system from practically anywhere.

Even though the centers are seldom in actual use for disaster recovery, they don't just sit there like a fire extinguisher in a glass case. All of them are manned by a technical staff that spends most of its time helping customers to implement and test their disaster-recovery procedures. In the event of an actual disaster, the staff is ready to provide immediate help with the recovery. As a result of the regularly scheduled tests that are a part of the service, they already have knowledge of the customer's operations. So there really is a significant service element to this business. The customer receives a lot more than just the right to rent a piece of hardware on a standby basis.

SunGard makes its service available only through term contracts, which run about 3 years on average and have historically been renewed at better than an 80% rate. This arrangement, of course, provides the basis for a highly predictable stream of recurring revenue, which gives the business good visibility and makes it more manageable.

The monthly rate on a very large mainframe system can run to more than $13,000. In the event that a subscriber needs to use the system for an actual disaster recovery, he must first pay a $25,000 declaration fee and then a daily usage fee in the range of $4,500–$8,000. These fees discourage customers from using the centers for processing overflow work and also offset SunGard's extra costs. However, they aren't high enough to allow much profit contribution, so frequency of use has essentially no impact on SunGard's earnings.

SunGard designed and built the world's first commercial disaster recovery center in 1978, and with approximately 500 subscribers it remains the leading company in the business today. Its customers include companies such as Westinghouse, NCNB National Bank, Northwestern Mutual Life, Public Service Electric & Gas Company, and RCA. Competition is essentially limited to Comdisco, a computer-leasing company. And given the prohibitively high cost of equipment and establishing a network, it's unlikely that anyone else will decide to enter the market.

Because there are about 3,000 IBM and IBM-compatible mainframe sites large enough to be likely candidates for disaster recovery services, this business has a long way to go before it reaches the saturation point. One factor that should help it continue to grow at a healthy clip is increasing awareness of just how necessary the service is. At the time of SunGard's initial public offering in March 1986, its system had never been used for an actual disaster recovery. The lack of use undoubtedly caused some prospective customers, not to mention investors, to wonder just how strong the need for it truly was. Then late that year Putnam Investor Services did put it to use. This was followed by four more successful recoveries in 1987. The fact that the system was called upon five times in less than 12 months validated the need for it, and undoubtedly helped a lot of potential customers gain a new appreciation of its importance. Here is how the president of Putnam Investor Services described his company's experience:

> Last December, an electrical fire in our headquarters building put our main computer center out of operation for a week. Fortunately, we had a contract with SunGard for disaster recovery services. In a very short time, we had restored operations at SunGard's Philadelphia facility. Our salesmen never stopped taking orders. (1986 annual report.)

Aside from the likelihood of deeper penetration, there are some other forces at work that should help SunGard keep growing rapidly. The potential market itself is still growing at a respectable rate. Not only is the population of large computer sites increasing, but more companies are becoming more computer-dependent, obviously a favorable trend. Also, SunGard is usually able to sell additional services to existing customers over time. And it benefits from provisions for 6% to 8% annual price increases in most of its contracts.

In addition to its disaster recovery services business, SunGard also sells data-processing services and software to the financial services industry. In this area it offers shareholder record-keeping and reporting systems for mutual funds and bank transfer agents, and a variety of accounting systems designed primarily for bank trust departments. Most customers elect to use SunGard's software on a remote processing basis under contracts that run 1 to 3 years. Because these contracts have experienced very

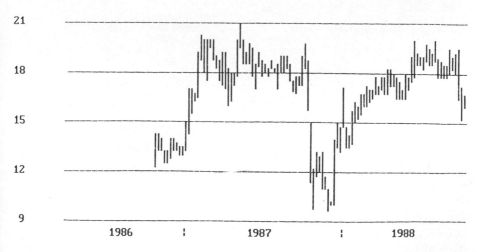

Figure 13.4. SunGard Data Systems, Inc. stock chart. Courtesy of Bridge Information Systems, Inc.

high renewal rates, this segment of the business enjoys the same recurring revenue aspect as disaster recovery services.

The financial services part of SunGard's business has benefited both from the proliferation of mutual fund products and increased government reporting requirements. However, its inherent growth rate is not as high as disaster recovery services, so the company has chosen to supplement its growth in this area with acquisitions. Although this is often a signal for caution, it's a strategy that seems to work better in the software industry than with other types of emerging growth companies. Certainly, this has been the case with Computer Associates, and so far with SunGard as well. One thing that has kept it out of trouble is that it concentrates on small companies whose characteristics mirror its own:

1. Dominance within a market niche.
2. High recurring revenue.
3. A strong service element.

As long as it sticks with these criteria and continues to limit itself to buying small companies in market segments it knows well, SunGard's acquisitive tendencies shouldn't be too much cause for concern. And in the meantime, its main business is a very attractive one, so it's well positioned to extend the record shown in Table 13.4.

TABLE 13.4 SunGard Data Systems Financial Summary ($000s omitted)

Year Ending 12/31	1985	1986	1987
Revenue	$58,586	$69,053	$91,118
Operating Margin	11.2%	15.1%	15.2%
Operating Income	6,570	10,436	13,876
Interest and Other Income, Net	373	1,002	1,252
Tax	3,131	5,948	6,913
Net Income from Operations	$ 3,812	$ 5,490	$ 8,215
Earnings per Share	$.51	$.64	$.81
Long-Term Debt	$ 2,402	$ 415	$16,445
Equity	18,133	35,340	71,022
Return on Average Equity	23.6%	20.5%	15.4%
Operating Cash Flow	$ 6,812	$10,494	$15,079
Working Capital Increase	(4,527)	3,348	4,087
Capital Expenditures	3,061	8,200	7,853
Surplus/(Deficit)	$ 8,278	$(1,054)	$ 3,139

CHAMBERS DEVELOPMENT COMPANY

You may remember one of those offbeat stories that captured the attention of the national media a year or two ago. A barge loaded with garbage left the Long Island Sound with plans to incinerate its cargo at sea. However, endless legal wrangling thwarted the original plan, and for months the barge searched for a port where it could unload the cargo for eventual disposal. It never did find one, and finally it ended its futile journey by returning home still loaded with the original cargo. If nothing else, the incident demonstrated how complex an issue waste disposal has become.

With greater awareness and concern for environmental consequences on the part of citizens and the government alike, it's no longer possible for municipalities and industry to simply dump waste in any uninhabited area. At the same time, many decrepit, poorly operated, overutilized land-fills are being closed. These closings, combined with a shortage of suitable land for new sites, have actually caused a decline in the number of per-mitted landfills, especially along the eastern seaboard.

As a result of these changes, waste management is no longer a prosaic, no-growth business; rather, it's a fragmented industry that presents a clas-sic opportunity for growth through consolidation. Chambers Develop-ment, an operator of solid waste landfills in Pennsylvania, North Carolina, and South Carolina, is among only a handful of companies with the man-agement and financial strength to take advantage of this opportunity. As the company points out in a recent annual report, the business demands increasing technical expertise that a lot of current participants simply don't have.

> The development and operation of a sanitary landfill is a complex, technically demanding and costly activity little understood by the general public. Effective landfills are engineered with clay or synthetic liners fol-lowing the excavation of a cell or section of land about to receive waste. Leachate collection and treatment facilities and groundwater monitoring devices are added to control the safety of the environment.
>
> Chambers maintains a fleet of bulldozers, scrapers, loaders, compac-tors, excavators and backhoes to construct and operate landfills. This heavy equipment is used to prepare a site and then to spread, compact and cover waste daily with earth or other approved material, creating lay-ers of compacted waste material and soil. The company then contours and revegetates a filled cell to prevent leaching and erosion and to create a natural appearance. . . .
>
> Prior to the purchase of these landfills, Chambers' staff of engineers tested the geology, hydrogeology and soil of each site and carefully ana-lyzed and evaluated environmental conditions.

Today the waste management industry is a fragmented, multibillion-dollar business. A few publicly owned companies control 20% or so of the market. The rest is split among thousands of municipalities and "mom and pop" operators whose lack of capital and technical expertise makes it increasingly difficult for them to keep up with ever-tightening environmental regulations. This makes it a business ripe for growth through consolidation.

The major asset that gives Chambers a favorable position within the industry is the large amount of permitted landfill capacity it controls, either under long-term leases or through outright ownership. As long as current trends continue, the supply and demand relationship will only get tighter; prices (called tipping fees) will increase further, as will the underlying value of the asset.

Ownership of landfill capacity also gives Chambers a significant edge in the more competitive, lower margin collection and handling segment of the business. Additionally, this part of the business is benefiting from a trend toward increased privatization. Some studies have shown private firms to be as much as 40% more efficient than municipal sanitation departments. This fact, coupled with budgetary pressures, is causing more and more municipalities to turn collection and handling over to the private sector.

The large amount of permitted landfill capacity under its control has also enabled Chambers to tie up an increasing amount of business with

TABLE 13.5 Chambers Development Company Financial Summary ($000s omitted)

Year Ending 12/31	1985	1986	1987
Revenue	$20,194	$31,443	$58,785
Operating Margin	22.2%	22.1%	22.0%
Operating Income	4,473	6,938	12,905
Interest and Other Income, Net	(260)	(79)	2,167
Tax	1,196	1,589	5,350
Net Income from Operations	$ 3,016	$ 5,270	$ 9,722
Earnings per Share	$.42	$.59	$.90
Long-Term Debt	$27,035	$71,568	$76,841
Equity	18,672	23,810	79,188
Return on Average Equity	23.1%	24.8%	18.9%
Operating Cash Flow	$ 5,428	$ 9,093	$16,820
Working Capital Increase	1,442	10	(53,058)
Capital Expenditures	14,040	26,968	51,855
Surplus/(Deficit)	$(10,054)	$(17,885)	$18,023

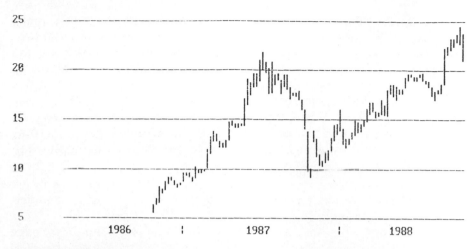

Figure 13.5. Chambers Development Company, Inc. stock chart. Courtesy of Bridge Information Systems, Inc.

long-term contracts. The prototype is an agreement with Passaic County, New Jersey, that began in 1988. Under this contract Chambers will accept solid waste from Passaic County until the county constructs its own incineration facilities, a project that is estimated to take about 5 years to complete. And even then, Chambers will continue to accept ash and material that cannot be incinerated—about 40% of the solid waste volume. Because the contract provides for Chambers to be paid in advance, it represents an important source of financing in a business that's very capital-intensive. And, of course, the contract also enlarges the company's recurring revenue base and enhances its visibility, which is already high because of the repeat nature of its service.

Increasing regulatory control of waste disposal operations has benefitted Chambers on balance, but it's also a source of risk. The company has reduced this risk through its policy of not handling hazardous waste. But there is always the chance of adverse regulatory developments disrupting business, even though Chambers is among the most competent and sophisticated operators. For instance, in the second half of 1987 the Pennsylvania Department of Environmental Resources announced a new program that prevented the company from taking additional business at any existing site without first going through a lengthy notice and hearing process. Although Chambers managed to get by this problem without any impact on its earnings, it's the kind of issue that can be expected to occur again.

Another drawback to Chambers' business is its high level of capital intensity. (See Table 13.5.) Landfills are expensive to develop and require a lot of equipment, as does the collection and hauling part of the business. To finance these requirements, Chambers has used various forms of borrowing, including the innovative prepayment feature of the Passaic County contract. But it's likely to remain dependent on external capital to finance a good portion of its growth.

In spite of this dependence and the potential vulnerability to regulatory changes, Chambers is well positioned to extend its impressive record. The company's recurring revenue base makes it manageable, and its competitive strength in a fragmented industry provides a good foundation for further growth.

14

Putting It All to Work

Early in my career as a securities analyst, the firm where I worked held regular meetings for all of the analysts and portfolio managers so we could share our best ideas. One day a fellow member of the research department gave a brief talk about a company whose stock he thought was a particularly attractive investment. As he described it, the outlook for this company's business seemed so good that it was hard to imagine any way it could miss having strong growth. The glowing description prompted one of the more acerbic portfolio managers to comment that his grandmother could probably do a good job of running this particular company. Of course he was being sarcastic, but it really didn't seem like that much of an exaggeration.

Later on it occurred to me that this was actually the key to growth stock investing. There may not be any companies that your grandmother could run, but there are some—like the five discussed in the last chapter— that are so well positioned to keep on growing that they certainly don't have to be run by a management genius. If you can invest in companies like these at prices that aren't outrageous, their growth is bound to increase the value of your portfolio over time. What could be a simpler or more appealing approach to investing?

Like any theory, this one is much easier to describe than put into practice. My purpose in this book has been to relate what has worked best and what has not worked at all, in my attempts. This can be distilled into a set

177

of 10 principles. As a favor to you for having read this far, I will overcome a great temptation and refrain from calling them the Ten Commandments of emerging growth investing. Anyway, here they are:

1. Stick with companies that

   • operate in an industry environment conducive to high growth;
   • have limited competition; and
   • are profitable enough to finance most of their growth internally.

If you find a company with these characteristics plus good management, so much the better. But don't count on your ability or anybody else's to judge managements.

2. Invest only in companies that have good visibility—preferably with a high base of recurring revenue. These companies are best able to cope with the enormous strains of high growth because they can anticipate future problems well in advance and plan with confidence. Because they are the easiest to keep under control and the least demanding to run, they are also the least likely to stumble and produce disappointing earnings.

3. Avoid companies that are hard to keep under control, particularly those that have long sales cycles, or are prone to inventory cycles, or are attempting to grow at a rate that seems unreasonably high.

4. Stay on the alert for companies that have the potential to increase their profit margins. These are the most likely to have favorable earnings surprises, gain higher multiples, and in the process turn into home-run stocks.

5. Think of your portfolio as an Ivy League college and yourself as the admissions director. There may be hundreds of qualified candidates, but you only have to accept a few of the best. The ability to be selective is one of the real advantages available to individual investors. Don't forfeit it by taking a passive approach to stock selection.

6. Be very cautious about the entire emerging growth sector of the market when the New Horizons Fund relative P/E is at or near 2.0x. At these points you should be very heavy in cash because multiple contraction can easily wipe out several years of strong earnings growth. Conversely, when the relative multiple is at 1.15x or less, you should be fully invested. There is good reason to believe that the same extremes in valua-

tion that have bounded the emerging growth sector since 1960 will continue to hold.

7. In judging the valuation of individual stocks, it's important to look beyond the relationship of growth to P/E. Often the best performing stocks in an emerging growth portfolio are those with the highest P/E ratios because they deliver earnings growth and don't disappoint investors. If you attempt to buy growth for the lowest possible P/E ratio, you'll usually end up with a portfolio full of junk. Principles that work well for value investors can't always be applied to emerging growth because it is such a different style.

8. Never forget that emerging growth stocks are usually illiquid and volatile. This can be very frustrating, but it can also create trading opportunities.

9. Try to ride your winners for as long as possible. You have to get a lot of mileage out of them to make up for the mistakes that are an inevitable part of emerging growth investing. But when a company's fundamentals turn sour, be a quick and ruthless seller. It is best to analyze the problems later on—from the sidelines.

10. Be patient. Emerging growth investing isn't easy; you'll make plenty of mistakes along the way. And the high returns necessary to compensate for above-average risk won't always come as quickly as you think they should.

All of these principles are intended to keep the risks of emerging growth under control and help you realize the very high returns these stocks are capable of providing over the long term. If this style of investing is new to you, you'll soon learn that watching small companies grow up can be exciting and a lot of fun, especially when you're participating in their growth as a shareholder.

Appendix

This appendix is included to provide readers with a starting point for defining the universe of emerging growth stocks. It furnishes the name, address, phone number, and a brief description of 200 companies. Most of these companies have annual revenue of less than $200 million and reasonably good growth records. However, the list also includes some companies, mostly in biotechnology, that are still in the development stage and do not yet have meaningful revenue, let alone earnings.

Many of the companies listed here also appear in one or more of the various lists of fastest growing companies mentioned in Chapter 3. You will find others in the portfolios of mutual funds that specialize in emerging growth. And still others are followed closely by the brokerage firms that have a serious research commitment to this sector of the market. So the list represents a kind of consensus of stocks that most knowledgeable investors would place in the emerging growth category. However, it is certainly not an exhaustive list, and it isn't intended to imply anything about the investment attractiveness of the stocks included in it. In fact, some of them lack the stock selection characteristics that I have advocated. And no doubt some of these stocks will turn out to be dogs, just as there are sure to be some winners that don't show up here. But the list does provide a good-sized initial pool of candidates to screen for possible inclusion in your portfolio.

A convenient way to quickly learn a little more about these stocks is to look them up in Standard & Poor's Stock Reports, which are available in many libraries and brokerage offices. These two page "tear sheets" capsulize a lot of pertinent information.

Once you've identified a company as a serious candidate, you'll want to write or call for annual and quarterly reports. Also be sure to request a 10-k. This form, which all public companies must file annually with the Securities and Exchange Commission, occasionally contains extra tidbits of information that can be helpful. Ask to be put on the mailing list, and request an information package. A lot of companies will send you reprints of articles and analysts' research reports. And last but not least, check with your broker to see what information he can supply.

Action Auto Rental
6830 Cochran Rd.
Solon, OH 44139
(216) 349-4440
Rents autos primarily for replacement purposes.

Acuson
1220 Charleston Rd.
Mountain View, CA 94039
(415) 969-9112
Manufactures ultrasound equipment for medical imaging.

Adobe Systems
1870 Embarcadero Rd.
Palo Alto, CA 94303
(415) 852-0271
Produces personal computer software for desktop publishing.

Advanced Marketing Services
4747 Morena Blvd.
San Diego, CA 92117
(619) 581-2232
Distributes books to membership warehouse clubs.

Aldus Corp.
411 First Ave. South
Seattle, WA 98104
(206) 622-5500
Produces personal computer software for desktop publishing.

Alliant Computer Systems
1 Monarch Dr.
Littleton, MA 01460
(617) 486-4950
Manufactures minisupercomputers for engineering and scientific applications.

Allwaste, Inc.
4800 Sugar Grove Blvd.
Stafford, TX 77477
(713) 240-0360
Provides environmental cleanup services.

American List
98 Cutter Mill Rd.
Great Neck, NY 11021
(516) 466-0602
Rents computerized lists of high-school students.

American Management Systems
1777 N. Kent St.
Arlington, VA 22209
(703) 841-6000
Provides software and systems engineering.

Amgen
1900 Oak Terrace Ln.
Thousand Oaks, CA 91320
(805) 499-3617
Uses recombinant DNA technology to develop biotech products.

Amplicon, Inc.
2020 East First St., Ste. 401
Santa Ana, CA 92705
(714) 834-0525
Leases and sells midrange computers via telemarketing.

Andover Controls
York & Haverhill Sts.
Andover, MA 01810
(617) 470-0555
Provides building automation systems.

Applied Biosystems
850 Lincoln Center Dr.
Foster City, CA 94404
(415) 570-6667
Manufactures equipment for biotech research.

Armor All Products
22 Corporate Park
Irvine, CA 92714
(714) 553-1003
Manufactures products for cleaning and protecting automobiles.

Autodesk
2320 Marinship Way
Sausalito, CA 94965
(415) 332-2344
Produces software for computer-aided design.

Ben & Jerry's Homemade, Inc.
Rte. 100, P. O. Box 240
Waterbury, VT 05676
(802) 244-5641
Manufactures and distributes superpremium ice cream.

Biocraft Laboratories
92 Route 46
Elmwood Park, NJ 07407
(201) 796-3434
Manufactures generic drugs.

Biogen, N. V.
14 Cambridge Center
Cambridge, MA 02142
(617) 864-8900
Develops biotech pharmaceuticals for AIDS, cancer, and other diseases.

Biomet, Inc.
P. O. Box 587
Warsaw, IN 46580
(219) 267-6639
Manufactures orthopedic implants.

Biotherapeutics, Inc.
357 Riverside Dr., P. O. Box 1676
Franklin, TN 37065
(615) 794-4700
Performs custom-tailored research for cancer patients.

Blockbuster Entertainment Corp.
901 E. Las Olas Blvd.
Fort Lauderdale, FL 33301
(305) 524-8200
Operates and franchises video rental stores.

BMR Financial Group, Inc.
2302 Parklake Dr., N.E., Ste. 200
Atlanta, GA 30345
(404) 934-9994
A bank holding company that also provides services to help other banks improve their profitability.

Bolar Pharmaceutical
130 Lincoln St.
Copiague, NY 11726
(516) 842-8383
Manufactures generic drugs.

Brand Companies, Inc.
1420 Renaissance Dr.
Park Ridge, IL 60068
(312) 298-1200
Provides asbestos removal services.

Calgene
1920 Fifth St.
Davis, CA 95616
(916) 753-6313
Develops biotech products for agricultural applications.

California Biotechnology
2450 Bayshore Frontage Rd.
Mountain View, CA 94043
(415) 966-1550
Develops biotech products for human therapeutics and drug delivery.

Canonie Environmental Services
800 Canonie Dr.
Porter, IN 46304
(219) 926-8651
Provides hazardous waste remediation services.

Casey's General Stores
1299 E. Broadway Ave.
Des Moines, IA 50313
(515) 263-3700
Operates a chain of convenience stores in small towns.

CCX Network
301 Industrial Blvd.
Conway, AR 72032
(501) 329-6836
Provides data-processing services for direct marketing.

CEM Corp.
P. O. Box 200
Matthews, NC 28106
(704) 821-7015
Manufactures microwave instrumentation for use in testing and analysis.

Centex Telemanagement, Inc.
185 Berry St., Bldg. 4, Ste. 2800
San Francisco, CA 94107
(415) 777-0477
Provides telecommunication management services to small- and medium-sized businesses.

Centocor, Inc.
244 Great Valley Pkwy.
Malvern, PA 19355
(215) 296-4488
Develops biotech products for diagnostic testing and therapeutics.

Ceradyne, Inc.
3169 Redhill Ave.
Costa Mesa, CA 92626
(714) 549-0421
Manufactures high-tech ceramic products.

Cerner Corp.
2800 Rockcreek Pkwy.
Kansas City, MO 64117
(816) 221-1024
Produces software for hospital management.

Cetus Corp.
1400 53rd St.
Emeryville, CA 94608
(415) 549-3300
Biotech company that focuses on therapeutic drugs.

Chambers Development
10700 Frankstown Rd.
Pittsburgh, PA 15235
(412) 242-6237
Provides waste management services.

Checkpoint Systems
550 Grove Rd., P. O. Box 188
Thorofare, NJ 08086
(609) 848-1800
Manufactures electronic article surveillance systems.

Chief Automotive Systems
1924 E. 4th St.
Grand Isle, NE 68802
(308) 384-9747
Manufactures systems for repairing auto bodies.

Chili's, Inc.
6820 LBJ Freeway, Ste. 200
Dallas, TX 75240
(214) 980-9917
Operates a chain of restaurants featuring
a casual, southwestern menu and atmosphere.

Chiron Corp.
4560 Horton St.
Emeryville, CA 94608
(415) 655-8730
Develops biotech products for diagnostic and therapeutic applications.

Ciprico, Inc.
2955 Xenium Ln.
Plymouth, MN 55441
(612) 559-2034
Manufactures intelligent disk controllers for computer systems.

Circle Fine Arts Corp.
875 N. Michigan Ave.
Chicago, IL 60611
(312) 943-0664
Operates a chain of contemporary art galleries.

Clayton Homes
P. O. Box 15169
Knoxville, TN 37901
(615) 970-7200
Manufactures housing.

Clean Harbors
325 Wood Rd.
Braintree, MA 02184
(617) 849-1800
Provides comprehensive environmental cleanup services.

Clothestime, Inc.
5325 E. Hunter Ave.
Anaheim, CA 92807
(714) 779-5881
Operates a chain of off-price young women's apparel stores.

Collagen Corp.
2455 Faber Pl.
Palo Alto, CA 94303
(415) 856-0200
Manufactures collagen-based products for tissue repair.

Commodore Environmental Services
150 E. 58th St., Ste. 3400
New York, NY 10155
(212) 308-5800
Provides asbestos removal services.

CompuTrac Inc.
222 Municipal Dr.
Richardson, TX 75080
(214) 234-4241
Produces software systems for law firms.

Continental Health Affiliates
900 Sylvan Ave.
Englewood Cliffs, NJ 07632
(201) 567-4600
Operates nursing homes and provides outpatient health care services.

Continental Medical Systems
650 Wilson Ln.
Mechanicsburg, PA 17055
(717) 691-8047
Operates medical rehabilitation facilities.

Cycare Systems, Inc.
4343 Camelback Rd., Ste. 320
Phoenix, AZ 85018
(602) 952-5300
Provides software systems for medical group practices.

Cypress Semiconductor
3901 N. First St.
San Jose, CA 95134
(408) 943-2600
Manufactures CMOS semiconductors.

Dallas Semiconductor
4350 Beltwood Pkwy. South
Dallas, TX 75244
(214) 450-0400
Manufactures specialty semiconductors.

Data Translation
100 Locke Dr.
Marlborough, MA 01752
(617) 481-3700
Manufactures image processing boards for personal computers.

Diagnostic Products
5700 W. 96th St.
Los Angeles, CA 90045
(213) 776-0180
Manufactures kits for the diagnosis of various diseases.

Diceon Electronics, Inc.
2500 Michelson Dr.
Irvine, CA 92714
(714) 833-0870
Manufactures complex, multilayer circuit boards.

Dionex Corp.
1228 Titan Way
Sunnyvale, CA 94088
(408) 737-0700
Manufactures ion chromotography systems.

Domain Technology
304 Turquoise St.
Milpitas, CA 95035
(408) 262-4100
Manufactures thin-film disks for data storage.

Dresher, Inc.
7200 S. Mason, P. O. Box 8
Bedford Park, IL 60499
(312) 594-8900
Manufactures brass beds and accessories.

Duquense Systems, Inc.
2 Allegheny Center
Pittsburgh, PA 15212
(412) 323-2600
Produces systems software for mainframe computers.

Durakon Industries
3200 Beecher Rd.
Flint, MI 48532
(313) 230-0633
Manufactures liners for pickup truckbeds.

ECAD, Inc.
2455 Augustine Dr.
Santa Clara, CA 95054
(408) 727-0264
Produces computer-aided engineering software for design of integrated circuits.

ECC International Corp.
175 Stafford Ave.
Stafford, PA 19087
(215) 687-2600
Manufactures computer systems used primarily for military training.

Egghead, Inc.
22027 17th Ave., S.E.
Bothell, WA 98021
(206) 486-7337
Operates a chain of software stores.

Elcotel, Inc.
6428 Parkland Dr.
Sarasota, FL 34243
(813) 758-0389
Manufactures and operates privately owned payphones.

EMC, Inc.
171 South St.
Hopkinton, MA 01748
(617) 435-1000
Manufactures products to improve the performance of midrange computer systems.

EMCON Associates
1921 Ringwood Ave.
San Jose, CA 95131
(408) 275-1444
Provides hazardous waste management services.

Enseco, Inc.
205 Alewife Brook Pkwy.
Cambridge, MA 02138

(617) 661-3111
Provides hazardous waste management services.

Entertainment Publications
1400 N. Woodward Ave.
Birmingham, MI 48011
(313) 642-8300
Publishes discount coupon books.

Environmental Control Group
Tall Oaks Corp. Center
1000 Lenola Rd.
Maple Shade, NJ 08052
(609) 866-1616
Provides asbestos removal services.

Environmental Systems
1015 Louisiana St.
Little Rock, AR 72202
(501) 376-8142
Provides hazardous waste treatment services.

Environmental Treatment &
Technologies Corp.
P. O. Box 551
Findlay, OH 45840
(419) 423-3529
Provides hazardous waste treatment services.

Envirosafe Services
900 E. 8th Ave.
King of Prussia, PA 19406
(215) 962-0800
Provides hazardous waste treatment services.

Excelan
2180 Fortune Dr.
San Jose, CA 95131
(408) 434-2300
Manufactures local area network products.

Expeditors International
19119 16th Ave. South
Seattle, WA 98121
(206) 246-3711
Forwards air freight.

E-Z-EM, Inc.
7 Portland Ave.
Westbury, NY 11590
(516) 333-8230
Produces diagnostic imaging products to assist radiologists.

First Financial Management Corp.
2695 Buford Hwy., N.E.
Atlanta, GA 30324
(404) 325-9715
Provides data-processing services for banks.

FIserv, Inc.
2152 S. 114th St.
Milwaukee, WI 53227
(414) 546-5000
Provides data-processing services for banks.

Flightsafety International
Marine Air Terminal
La Guardia Airport
Flushing, NY 11371
(718) 565-4100
Uses simulators to provide training courses for professional pilots.

Flow Systems, Inc.
21440 68th Ave. South
Kent, WA 98206
(206) 356-5310
Manufactures ultra-high-velocity water jet cutting systems.

Forest Labs
150 E. 58th St.
New York, NY 10155
(212) 421-7850
Manufactures drugs incorporating controlled release dosage technology.

Frequency Electronics, Inc.
50 Charles Lindberg Blvd.
Mitchel Field, NY 11553
(516) 794-4500
Manufactures defense electronics products.

Fur Vault
360 W. 31st St.
New York, NY 10001
(212) 563-7070
Operates a chain of retail fur stores.

Gaming and Technology
3101 W. Spring Mountain Rd.
Las Vegas, NV 89102
(702) 732-2672
Operates gaming machine routes in Nevada.

General Parametrics
1250 9th St.
Berkeley, CA 94710
(415) 524-3950
Produces graphic presentation products for personal computers.

Gen-Probe, Inc.
9880 Campus Point Dr.
San Diego, CA 92121
(619) 546-8000
Develops medical products based on genetic probe technology.

Geraghty & Miller, Inc.
125 E. Bethpage Rd.
Plainview, NY 11803
(516) 249-7600
Provides environmental cleanup services.

Golden Valley Microwave Foods
7450 Metro Blvd.
Edina, MN 55435
(612) 835-6900
Sells popcorn and other food products for preparation in microwave ovens.

Greenery Rehabilitation Group
215 1st St.
Cambridge, MA 02142
(617) 824-7200
Operates rehabilitation hospitals.

Groundwater Technology
220 Norwood Park South
Norwood, MA 02062
(617) 769-7600
Provides environmental cleanup services.

Group 1 Software
6404 Ivy Ln.
Greenbelt, MD 20770
(301) 982-2000
Provides mail management software for IBM mainframe computers.

Grundle Environmental Systems
1340 E. Richey Rd.
Houston, TX 77073
(713) 443-8564
Manufactures and installs systems to prevent groundwater contamination.

GTECH Corp.
101 Dyer St.
Providence, RI 02903
(401) 273-7700
Designs and operates state lottery systems.

Healthcare Services Group
2643 Huntingdon Pike
Huntingdon Valley, PA 19006
(215) 938-1661
Provides housekeeping and linen services for nursing homes.

HEALTHSOUTH Rehabilitation
Two Perimeter Park South
Birmingham, AL 35243
(205) 967-7116
Provides medical rehabilitation services.

HEICO Corp.
3000 Taft St.
Hollywood, FL 33021
(305) 987-6101
Manufactures health care and aerospace equipment.

Home Office Reference Laboratory
10310 W. 84th Terrace
Lenexa, KS 66214
(913) 888-8397
Provides blood and urine tests for the life insurance industry.

Immunex Corp.
51 University St.
Seattle, WA 98101
(206) 587-0430
Develops immune-system-related biotech products.

Inacomp Computer Centers
1824 W. Maple Rd.
Troy, MI 48084
(313) 649-0910
Operates and franchises computer stores.

Informix Corp.
4100 Bohanon Dr.
Menlo Park, CA 94025
(415) 322-4100
Provides data-base management and other software systems.

InSpeech
2570 Blvd. of the Generals
P. O. Box 928
Valley Forge, PA 19482
(215) 631-9300
Provides speech and physical therapy services.

Integrated Device Technology
3236 Scott Blvd.
Santa Clara, CA 95051
(408) 727-6116
Manufactures CMOS semiconductors.

Integrated Genetics
51 New York Ave.
Framingham, MA 01701
(617) 875-1336
Develops therapeutic and diagnostic biotech products.

Interleaf
10 Canal Park
Cambridge, MA 02141
(617) 577-9800
Produces systems and software for computer-aided publishing.

Intertrans Corp.
8505 Freeport Pkwy.
Irving, TX 75063
(214) 929-8888
Forwards air freight.

Invitron Corp.
4649 Le Bourget Dr.
St. Louis, MO 63134
(314) 426-5000
Biotech firm that specializes in mammalian cell culture systems.

Isomedix Corp.
11 Apollo Dr.
Whippany, NJ 07981
(201) 887-4700
Provides irradiation services for sterilization.

Jiffy Lube International
6000 Metro Dr.
Baltimore, MD 21215
(301) 764-3555
Franchises and operates quick lube service centers.

Juno Lighting, Inc.
2001 S. Prospect Rd.
Des Plaines, IL 60017
(312) 827-9880
Manufactures recessed and track lighting fixtures.

KLA Instruments
2051 Mission College Blvd.
Santa Clara, CA 95054
(408) 988-6100
Manufactures optical testing equipment for the semiconductor industry.

Komag, Inc.
591 Yosemite Dr.
Milpitas, CA 95035
(408) 946-2300
Manufactures thin film disks for data storage.

Lam Research
47531 Warm Springs Blvd.
Fremont, CA 94539
(415) 659-0200
Manufactures equipment for the semiconductor industry.

Land's End, Inc.
8420 West Bryn Mawr Ave.
Chicago, IL 60631
(312) 693-0520
Does direct mail marketing of preppy apparel.

La Petite Academy
P. O. Box 26610
Kansas City, MO 64196
(816) 474-4750
Operates preschool and day-care centers.

Linear Technology
1630 McCarthy Blvd.
Milpitas, CA 95035
(408) 432-1900
Manufactures linear semiconductors.

The Liposome Co., Inc.
1 Research Way
Princeton Forrestal Center
Princeton, NJ 08540
(609) 452-7060
Develops liposome technology for drug delivery.

McGrath Rent Corp.
10760 Bigge St.
San Leandro, CA 94577
(415) 568-8866
Rents and sells modular offices to fulfill temporary needs.

MacNeal-Schwendler Corp.
815 Colorado Blvd.
Los Angeles, CA 90041
(213) 258-9111
Provides software for computer-aided engineering.

Mail Boxes, Etc.
5555 Oberlin Dr.
San Diego, CA 92121
(619) 452-1553
Franchises stores that provide postal and business services.

Matrix Science Corp.
455 Maple Ave.
Torrance, CA 90503
(213) 328-0271
Manufactures electronic connectors.

Med Chem Products, Inc.
43 Nagog Park
Action, MA 01720
(617) 263-8041
Manufactures biomedical products.

Medco Containment Services
491 Edward H. Ross Dr.
Elmwood Park, NJ 07407
(201) 794-1000
Distributes prescription drugs through mail order.

Medicine Shoppe International
1100 N. Lindbergh
St. Louis, MO 63132
(314) 993-6000
Franchises pharmacies.

Mentor Corp.
600 Pine Ave.
Santa Barbara, CA 93117
(805) 967-3451
Manufactures implantable medical devices and condoms.

Merrill Corp.
1 Merrill Circle
St. Paul, MN 55108
(612) 646-4501
Provides printing services to financial, legal, and corporate markets.

MicroAge, Inc.
2308 S. 55th St.
Tempe, AZ 85282
(602) 968-3168
Franchises computer stores.

MMI Medical
1900 Royalty Dr.
Pomona, CA 91767
(714) 620-0391
Provides diagnostic imaging services with mobile units.

MNX, Inc.
5310 St. Joseph Ave.
St. Joseph, MO 64505
(816) 233-3158
Long-haul truckload motor carrier.

Morino Associates
8615 Westwood Center Dr.
Vienna, VA 22180
(703) 734-9494
Provides software for IBM mainframe computers.

M. S. Carriers
3150 Starnes Cove
Memphis, TN 38116
(901) 332-2500
Irregular route truckload motor carrier.

Mylan Laboratories
1030 Century Building
Pittsburgh, PA 15222
(412) 232-0100
Manufactures generic drugs.

Nellcor, Inc.
25495 Whitesell St.
Hayward, CA 94545
(415) 887-5858
Manufactures instruments for blood gas monitoring.

Neutrogena Corp.
5755 W. 96th St.
Los Angeles, CA 90045
(213) 642-1150
Manufactures premium-priced soap and skin care products.

New England Critical Care
165 Forest St.
Marlborough, MA 01752
(617) 480-0503
Provides home infusion therapy services.

Newport Corp.
18235 Mt. Baldy Circle
Fountain Valley, CA 92708
(714) 963-9811
Manufactures laser accessories.

Novametrix Medical Systems
1 Barnes Industrial Park
Wallingford, CT 06492
(203) 265-7701
Manufactures medical electronic systems.

Nova Pharmaceutical
6200 Freeport Centre
Baltimore, MD 21224
(301) 522-7000
Develops new drugs and delivery systems.

Octel Communications
890 Tasman Dr.
Milpitas, CA 95035
(408) 942-6500
Manufactures voice processing systems.

One Price Clothing
290 Commerce Park, Hwy. 290
Duncan, SC 29334
(803) 439-6666
Operates off-price women's apparel stores.

On-Line Software Int., Inc.
2 Executive Park
Fort Lee, NJ 07024
(201) 592-0009
Produces software for mainframe computer systems.

Optical Radiation
1300 Optical Dr.
Azusa, CA 91702
(818) 969-3344
Manufactures intraocular lenses and optical components.

Pansophic Systems
709 Enterprise Dr.
Oak Brook, IL 60521
(312) 986-6000
Produces software for mainframe computers.

Par Pharmaceutical, Inc.
1 Ram Ridge
Spring Valley, NY 10977
(914) 425-7100
Manufactures generic drugs.

Paychex, Inc.
911 Panorama Trail South
Rochester, NY 14625
(716) 385-6666
Provides computerized payroll accounting services.

PCS, Inc.
9060 E. Via Linda
Scottsdale, AZ 85258
(602) 391-4600
Provides computer-based prescription claims processing.

Pentech International
999 New Durham Rd.
Edison, NJ 08817
(201) 287-6640
Manufactures pens and markers.

Policy Management Systems
1321 Lady St.
Columbia, SC 29201
(803) 748-2000
Produces software systems for the insurance industry.

Polk Audio
5601 Metro Dr.
Baltimore, MD 21215
(301) 358-3600
Manufactures high-quality stereo speakers.

QMS, Inc.
57 S. Schillinger Rd.
Mobile, AL 36608
(205) 343-2767
Manufactures computer printers and equipment.

Radiation Systems
1501 Moran Rd.
Sterling, VA 22170
Manufactures antenna products for commercial satellites and other communication markets.

REFAC Technology Development
122 E. 42nd St.
New York, NY 10168
(212) 687-4741
Manufactures electronic products.

Richardson Electronics
40W267 Keslinger Rd.
La Fox, IL 60147
(312) 232-6400
Manufactures and distributes electronic components.

RLI Corp.
9025 N. Lindberg Dr.
Peoria, IL 61615
(309) 692-1000
Provides contact lens replacement insurance.

Ryan's Family Steak Houses
2711 Wade Hampton Blvd.
Greenville, SC 29615
(803) 879-1000
Operates and franchises restaurants.

SafeCard Services
6400 N.W. 6th Way
Ft. Lauderdale, FL 33309
(305) 491-2111
Provides services to credit card holders.

Sahlen & Associates
700 W. Hillsboro Blvd.
Deerfield Beach, FL 33441
(305) 429-3301
Provides security services.

Salick Health Care
407 N. Maple Dr.
Beverly Hills, CA 90210
(213) 276-0732
Operates cancer treatment and kidney dialysis centers.

Satellite Music Network
12655 N. Central Expwy.
Dallas, TX 75243
(214) 991-9200
Supplies radio programming via satellite.

Sbarro, Inc.
763 Larkfield Rd.
Commack, NY 11725
(516) 864-0200
Operates a chain of family-style Italian restaurants.

SCI Systems, Inc.
5000 Technology Dr.
Huntsville, AL 35805
(205) 882-4800
Manufactures subassemblies for personal computer manufacturers.

Sigma Designs
46501 Landing Pkwy.
Fremont, CA 94538
(415) 770-0100
Manufactures products that enhance the performance of personal computers.

Silicon Graphics
2011 Stierlin Rd.
Mountain View, CA 94039
(415) 960-1980
Manufactures high performance workstations for design and analysis of 3-D objects.

Silk Greenhouse
1401 Tampa East Blvd.
Tampa, FL 33619
(816) 622-7886
Operates a chain of stores specializing in artificial flowers and decorating accessories.

Software Publishing Corp.
1901 Landings Dr.
Mountain View, CA 94043
(415) 962-8910
Provides business software for personal computers.

Spec's Music
1666 N.W. 82nd Ave.
Miami, FL 33126

(305) 592-7288
Operates a chain of record and video stores.

Stockholder Systems
4411 E. Jones Bridge Rd.
Norcross, GA 30092
(404) 441-3387
Provides financial applications software for IBM mainframes.

Stratus Computer, Inc.
55 Fairbanks Blvd.
Marlboro, MA 01752
(617) 460-2000
Manufactures fault-tolerant computers.

Structural Dynamics Research
2000 Eastman Dr.
Milford, OH 45150
(513) 576-2400
Provides computer-aided engineering software and services for designing
mechanical products.

SunGard Data Systems
1285 Drummers Ln.
Wayne, PA 19087
(215) 341-8700
Performs disaster recovery services for large computer facilities.

Surgical Care Affiliates
4515 Harding Rd.
Nashville, TN 37205
(615) 385-3541
Operates outpatient surgical care centers.

Symbol Technologies, Inc.
116 Wilbur Pl.
Bohemia, NY 11716
(516) 563-2400
Manufactures laser scanning equipment.

Synbiotics Corp.
11011 Via Frontera

San Diego, CA 92127
(619) 451-3770
Develops monoclonal antibodies for human and veterinary products.

Synergen, Inc.
1885 33rd St.
Boulder, CO 80301
(303) 938-6200
Develops biotech products with recombinant DNA and other techniques.

Systematics, Inc.
4001 Rodney Parham Rd.
Little Rock, AR 72212
(501) 223-5100
Performs data processing services for banks.

System Software Associates
500 W. Madison St., 32nd Fl.
Chicago, IL 60606
(312) 641-2900
Produces business applications software.

TCA Cable TV
3015 SSE Loop 323
P. O. Box 130489
Tyler, TX 75713
(214) 595-3701
Operates classic cable systems in small markets.

TCBY Enterprises
11300 Rodney Parham Rd.
Little Rock, AR 72212
(501) 688-8229
Franchises frozen yogurt stores.

Telecredit
1901 Ave. of the Stars
Los Angeles, CA 90067
(213) 277-4061
Provides check authorization and credit card processing services.

Telematics International
1415 N. W. 62nd St.
Fort Lauderdale, FL 33309
(305) 772-3070
Manufactures equipment for wide area data networks.

Telos Corp.
3420 Ocean Park Blvd.
Santa Monica, CA 90405
(213) 450-2424
Performs software design and consulting for defense and space programs.

Telxon Corp.
3330 W. Market St.
Akron, OH 44313
(216) 867-3300
Manufactures portable teletransaction computer systems.

TEMPEST Technologies
460 Herndon Pkwy.
Herndon, VA 22070
(703) 471-0157
Modifies computer systems to comply with government security services.

Teradata Corp.
12945 Jefferson Blvd.
Los Angeles, CA 90066
(213) 827-8777
Manufactures high performance fault-tolerant computer systems.

Thrifty Rent-A-Car System
4608 South Garnett Rd.
Tulsa, OK 74146
(918) 665-3930
Daily car rental firm with off-airport locations.

Timberline Software
9405 S.W. Gemini
Beaverton, OR 97005
(503) 626-6775
Produces accounting and information management software.

T. Rowe Price Associates, Inc.
100 E. Pratt St.
Baltimore, MD 21202
(301) 547-2000
Provides money management services and sponsors mutual funds.

Total Systems Services
1000 5th Ave., P. O. Box 120
Columbus, GA 31902
(404) 649-2387
Provides bankcard and other data-processing services for banks.

Uniforce Temporary Personnel, Inc.
1335 Jerricho Tpk.
New Hyde Park, NY 11040
(516) 437-3300
Operates temporary personnel agencies.

Uni-Marts, Inc.
477 E. Beaver Ave.
State College, PA 16801
(814) 234-6000
Operates a chain of convenience stores.

United Education & Software, Inc.
15720 Ventura Blvd.
Encino, CA 91436
(213) 872-3701
Operates a chain of career and home study schools.

UTL Corp.
4500 W. Mockingbird Ln.
Dallas, TX 75209
(214) 350-7601
Produces electronic systems for radar reconnaissance.

Vanguard Technologies
1 Flint Hill, Ste. 300
10530 Rosehaven St.
Fairfax, VA 22030
(703) 273-0500
Provides data-processing services to government agencies.

Varitronic Systems
600 S. Country Rd. 18
Minneapolis, MN 55426
(612) 542-1500
Manufactures print-on-tape lettering systems.

V Band Corp.
5 O'Dell Plaza
Yonkers, NY 10701
(914) 964-0900
Produces high-density electronic telephone systems.

Vestar, Inc.
939 E. Walnut St.
Pasadena, CA 91106
(818) 792-6101
Developes liposome technology for drug delivery.

Vipont Pharmaceuticals
1625 Sharp Point Dr.
Fort Collins, CO 80525
(303) 482-3126
Manufactures oral hygiene products.

Werner Enterprises
I-80 & Hwy. 50
Omaha, NE 68138
(402) 895-6640
Truckload motor vehicle carrier.

Weston (Roy F.), Inc.
Weston Way
West Chester, PA 19380
(215) 692-3030
Provides hazardous waste management services.

Williams-Sonoma, Inc.
100 N. Point St.
San Francisco, CA 94133
(415) 421-7900
Specialty retailer of cooking and gardening equipment.

Xylogics, Inc.
53 3rd Ave.
Burlington, MA 01803
(617) 272-8140
Manufactures electronic equipment to control the flow of data in computer systems.

Index